BODY
REFLEXOLOGY

BODY REFLEXOLOGY

Healing
at Your
Fingertips

Mildred Carter

PARKER PUBLISHING COMPANY
WEST NYACK, NEW YORK

This book is a reference work based on research by
the author. The opinions expressed herein are not
necessarily those of or endorsed by the publisher.
The directions stated in this book are in no way
to be considered as a substitute for consultation
with a duly licensed doctor.

Library of Congress Cataloging in Publication Data

Carter, Mildred.
Body reflexology.

Includes index.
1. Reflexology. I. Title.
RM723.R43C37 1983   615.8'22   83-2422
ISBN 0-13-079699-9
ISBN 0-13-079681-6 {PBK}
26 27 28 29 30
25 26 27 28 29 30   (PBK)

PRINTED IN THE UNITED STATES OF AMERICA

Appreciation

Thanks to my family and friends and the many chiropractors, naturopathic physicians and medical doctors who have given their time and support in helping me complete this book.

Thanks to Stirling Enterprises, Inc., Cottage Grove, Oregon, for use of the reflex devices that were used as models.

And my special thanks to Margaret Roe for her invaluable help in typing the manuscript.

Also by Mildred Carter

Helping Yourself with Foot Reflexology
Hand Reflexology: Key to Perfect Health

A Word from the Author

HOW YOU CAN FEEL GOOD ALL OVER
AND HELP YOUR BODY STOP MOST PAIN
ALMOST INSTANTLY

Reflexology is a sensational, dynamic, yet simple approach to glowing health! Through reflex massage you will be able to eliminate the causes and symptoms of sickness and pain from your whole body.

Your body is a temple. It is energy, held together by the same force that holds the stars and the moon and the sun in their places. Your body is controlled by an electrical system with many on-and-off switches. There are main circuits to every organ, gland, and nerve in your body, and these circuits have endings in your hands and feet. But they can also be tapped in various parts of the body.

By massaging reflexes in various places on the body, you not only stop pain but you also send a healing force to all parts of the body by opening up closed electrical lines that have shut off the universal life force. When these life lines are clogged, malfunctioning glands and organs make you ill. Reflexology is simple and safe for anyone to use, anywhere and at any time. The dynamic healing forces of reflexology can make you whole, can bring vigor, vitality, and beauty back into your life, and can help keep you free from illness and pain for the rest of your long life.

I have spent the past few years traveling throughout the world and studying every method of natural healing that was available to me so that I might pass it on to you.

I have learned many marvelous things about healing the body, making it beautiful, and renewing interest in life. To be healthy is to live joyfully. No one knows this better than those who have suffered from pain and poor health for most of their lives.

Reflexology is truly magic, but you don't need a magician to make it work for you or for anyone else. It is all right there in your hands. So please use it today and every day for a happy, pain-free life for yourself and for all those you want to free from pain and illness!

From the time when I was a small child, I had a great desire to heal. If someone was in pain or ill, I felt that I should be able to pass my hand over him or her and make all pain and illness vanish. I couldn't understand why this wouldn't work.

As a grown-up, I have almost been able to accomplish this desire. I have discovered that there is a force within us that can heal: we can reach out with our hands and send a healing radiation surging into the energy field of another person. Most of us, however, have not developed this power to its full capacity. In this book I will tell you how you can use your power through reflexology to heal yourself and others and realize almost instant results, no matter who you are.

Reflexology is truly the healing miracle of the new age we are entering. Hopefully, reflexology will be taught someday in all the schools all over the world, when love and compassion outweigh the greed of nations. Then health will be returned to the land.

In this book you will learn methods that will stop headaches, toothaches, and backaches within minutes, not only for yourself but also for your friends and loved ones. These methods relieve constipation, sore throat, shortness of breath, heart pains, stomach problems, hiccups, earache, sciatica, hemorrhoids, childbirth pains, colds, and flu. Body reflexology methods also overcome problems of endocrine glands, failing kidneys, and the liver. These methods bring help to those suffering from asthma, colon problems, and arthritis. You will learn how to have beautiful breasts, how to become beautiful with a reflexology face lift, and how to overcome sexual impotency.

Body reflexology also lets you detect health problems before they become serious. You will gain more youthful energy and discover how to reduce health-destroying mental and physical tensions. These simple methods can be applied at any time and practically anywhere. When a headache attacks you at an inopportune time, such as at a business meeting, at a party, or in a conference, you can stop it immediately.

You will learn how to take a reflex break for a fast pickup of energy wherever you might be—working in the office, shopping in a store, driving a car, or when the kids seem to be too much for you to handle.

Reflex massage starts the calmative action that brings relief to tense nerves and knotted muscles. Within minutes, it banishes fatigue and sends a new vitality pulsing through your whole body. Reflex massage encourages the flow of blood and enables the blood vessels to bathe the tissue cells directly. It seems to create a greater flow of blood throughout the body without undue strain, pressure, or overexertion of the heart. Thus, reflexology assists in the healthful nourishment of the body.

Using the methods described in my previous books, thousands of men, women, and children, in just one or two treatments, have been relieved of pain and illness that had plagued them for many years. Now I bring you body reflexology. This book tells you how to use reflex buttons all over your head and body.

In all my studies of many natural methods of healing, I have never found one that compares with reflexology in bringing relief from most ailments. Yet reflexology is still unknown to too many people. I wish there were some way that I could tell everyone in the world about this wonderful, natural, harmless way to complete health. Those who have discovered the wonderful healing power of reflex massage tell me of really unbelievable cures that they and their friends have obtained.

No one should depend completely on reflexology as a cure-all. There are times when a doctor may be needed. But reflexology is a simple, harmless method of treating many illnesses. I do not believe that people were made to live with illnesses and pain. A person is a structural, chemical, and spiritual being, and you will learn to bring the structural, the chemical, and the spiritual into balance so that you can treat the whole body. If every part of the body is not in balance and there is one tiny place that is malfunctioning, there can be no complete relief from pain and illness.

Reflexology gets to the cause of a body malfunction by restoring the energy flow to the body's many different systems and functions. I will show you how to massage the reflexes on certain parts of your body to tap the healing current and to bring natural and prompt relief from practically all aches and pains, chronic or acute. Other books on body reflex massage that I have read have been rather complex and hard to understand. Here you will find the techniques of body reflex massage fully and simply illustrated by diagrams and photographs. Because I wish to keep this method of self-help easy to learn, I will use only the important reflexes that I feel will be of the most benefit to you. Body reflexology requires no expense, no special equipment, no drugs or medication.

By looking at the table of contents you will see the wide range of situations in which body reflexology has been used to obtain beneficial results.

Note: Photos appear on pages 65-94.

—Mildred Carter

Table of Contents

Women • Massage of the Arms and Legs • The Back • Using Reflex Tongue Probe • Overcoming Impotency in Men • Your Voice Affects Your Masculine Vitality • Reflexology to Build Healthy Sex Organs in the Male • How to Help a Stubborn Case of Prostate Trouble • How to Be a Great Lover • How to Convert Sex Energy into Finer Forces • How to Use Reflexology for Painless Childbirth

Using Foot Reflexes • Using Hand Reflexes • Reflexes of the Heel Pad

Using Body Reflexes for Asthma • Reflexes to the Adrenal Gland • An Additional Help for Asthmatics • Reflexology Helps Emphysema • Music Helps the Breath

Using Hand Reflexes • Exploring the Tongue • Help for Other Symptoms

Using Hand Reflexes • Using Foot Reflexes • Dealing with Frequent Headaches • Other Methods for Headaches • How to Cure a Migraine Headache • Fainting or Dizzy Spells

Reflex Foot Massager • Reflex Roller Massager • Reflex Hand Probe • Magic Reflex Massager • Tongue Cleaner • Palm Massager • Reflex Comb • Reflex Clamps • Tongue Depressor or Probe • Wire Brush Stimulates Reflexes • The Miracle of the Miniature Trampoline • Bed Raisers

The Importance of Being Beautiful • An Aid to Skin Beauty • A Do-It-Yourself Face Lift at Home • A Touch for Beauty • Help for Acne

I

How Reflexology Works to Help the Body Heal Itself

More than ten million Americans have seen the effectiveness of reflexology on TV and have read of this natural technique of healing in many national magazines as well as in most newspapers. It is sometimes described under different names, but all of these methods use the technique of pressing on certain points of the body.

I have proved beyond any doubt whatsoever the healing power of reflex massage in my books *Hand Reflexology: Key to Perfect Health* and *Helping Yourself with Foot Reflexology.*

Now we will take you a step further with the wonders of body massage which will also bring miracles of healing into your life and the lives of those you love.

Body reflexology will start the functioning of many processes throughout the whole body and leave nothing unattended when you follow the directions given.

You will release the healing power of the lymphatic system by opening up the flow of lymph fluid into damaged areas. You will speed up the healing forces by activating the nervous system when you massage the reflexes as directed, and balance the vital energies among all the various systems.

Glance for a moment at Diagram 1. Notice how energy and circulation are slowed down when there is blockage in the line. We start health flowing back into our bodies by breaking up this blockage and letting the life energy flow freely to all parts of the body.

A tender spot any place on your body indicates a point of congestion in the energy lines, which in turn means trouble in some area that may be far removed from the tender point.

Now you can see why reflexology works such miracles of healing. This simple miracle of magic healing has been overlooked for many years because of its very simplicity.

17

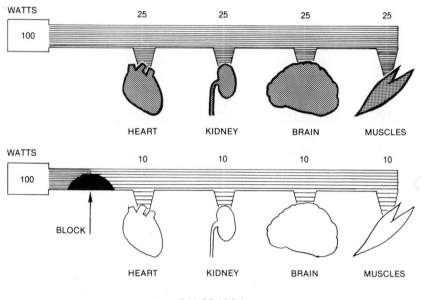

DIAGRAM I

A Medical Doctor Is Convinced

Mrs. Carter's explanation of why her reflexology works clashes so much with what I or any other physician who has studied the nervous system believe, that my first reaction to her book was anything but positive. But then I remembered the wisdom of a saying, "Why something works is not as important as whether it does work." The "whys" of any working method can be changed, but no "why" can help any *not-working* method to perform.

So, I put Mrs. Carter to the test of trying reflexology on several people and found, to my surprise, that everything in her book was verified. Now I do not doubt the efficacy of this method.

—Dr. Van S.

HOW REFLEXOLOGY WORKS

The press of a finger on a certain "button" (nerve ending) on the body may result in an odd tingling sensation in quite a different area, and you will know that the reflex button is connected with this remote part. Hold it for a few seconds; if it is sensitive, press it several times. You now have proof that the healing massage of the reflex is getting through to the source of the trouble.

Sometimes the tingling will be felt where you least expect it. This doesn't always happen, but when it does you will be aware that you have discovered a life-giving current of health. It is this reward that makes reflex massage so valuable. It covers all parts of the body and brings them under control. It keeps corrosion from forming and causing trouble later on.

Don't be impatient. You must keep in mind that it has taken a long time for you to get into your present condition. Now you must give nature some time to correct it, although often the improvement is so rapid that it does seem like a miracle.

In some cases it is necessary to use prolonged stimulation to alleviate the pain, sometimes from twenty minutes to an hour. So don't give up if the pain does not subside immediately. It will work!

TREAT THE SLIGHTEST TWINGE OF PAIN

Whenever you feel a pain anywhere in your body, even the sightest twinge of a pain, no matter where it is located, press and massage it *immediately*! It is the body's method of sending you a signal via the reflexes that there is trouble. Someplace there is a blockage causing malfunctioning to a certain area in the body. It may be far removed from the messenger sending the signal, but press the button now and you may prevent future illness from striking unexpectedly later on. Always listen to your body. You will always get a warning signal before illness strikes, so heed it as you would a red light at a street crossing. *Stop* and press the reflex button, and you will continue to live free from illness.

SCIENTIFIC EVIDENCE THAT REFLEXOLOGY WORKS

Ever since oriental acupuncture was introduced to the western world, interested doctors have sought to find scientific proof that stimulation of certain points in the body stops pain and helps heal illnesses. (By scientific proof we mean that which is obtained under controlled laboratory conditions.)

Recent research in France, Scotland, Canada, the United States, and other western countries has produced a number of discoveries that throw light on the way reflexology as well as acupuncture may produce an effect.

Dr. Roger Dalet, a specialist at Beaujon Hospital in Paris, tells us in his book, *How to Give Yourself Relief from Pain by the Simple Pressure of a Finger,* that stimulation of certain acupuncture points (which are the same as reflexology points) causes the blood to become enriched and causes a marked improvement in respiratory function, particularly in asthmatic patients. Patients with disturbed heart rhythms show a marked improvement after acupuncture.

Dr. Dalet goes on to describe recordings of the movements of the stomach and intestines, called peristalsis. These have revealed that when peristalsis has been excessive—which may become very painful—the application of acupuncture needles in the front of the abdomen has brought about a considerable reduction of activity and a general calming of the system.

In this book I will show you how to accomplish the same results by using pressure on certain points instead of the acupuncture needles.

SCIENCE EXPLAINS WHY REFLEXOLOGY WORKS

The reflex points are energy junctions that relay and reinforce energy along meridian lines of the body, passing energy toward the organs and the nervous system.

Dr. Becker and his colleagues have been experimenting and testing with electrodes and have come up with scientific proof that electrical current passes most readily along the body's meridian lines. This proves that there are specific electrical properties at the reflex points and along the meridians that are different from the surrounding tissues.

After many months of testing at Aberdeen University and the University of California at La Jolla, a series of chemical messengers in the brain, chemically very similar to the drug morphine, were discovered. These have been called endorphines and they have the same effect as morphine in suppressing pain. They seem to work by blocking the transmission of pain impulses from one neuron to another.

A number of these substances, all rather similar chemically, have now been discovered. They are known to have a calming or even euphoric effect, producing optimism and even joy, according to their chemical structure and the part of the brain affected.

A Canadian scientist, Professor Pomeranz of Toronto, made the discovery that acupuncture liberated these very endorphines. Reflexology accomplishes the same effect using pressure instead of needles.

MANY HAVE BEEN HELPED

I have received hundreds of letters from people all over the world telling of sensational cures of nearly every type of illness using reflex massage. Here are letters from two who were helped.

Body Massage Helped an Eighty-three-year-old

Dear Mrs. Carter,

I want to tell you about the wonderful results I am having with body massage. I am eighty-three years young, and thanks to you, my dear, I am young. Before you told me about the reflexes in the body I was hardly able to get around. I didn't have enough strength to get enough pressure on my feet and hands, although it did help some. I decided to try your complete method of massaging the reflexes in my body and, praise God, I could do it and feel the results. I just put all of my fingers together on both hands and pressed in deep where I needed relief, which was in most of my body. I could actually feel the healing working. How wonderful reflexology is and how wonderful I feel again. I think I will find a young husband!

I am sure you were placed on this earth to help God's people who are so in need of his natural methods of healing. Keep it up, my prayers are with you.

—Mrs. N. M.

Letter from a Minister

Dear Mrs. Carter,

I want to tell you what I have done with reflexology. After my sermon one Sunday I told my congregation that I was going to show those who were interested how to regain their health and keep it by using natural methods. I had everyone massage certain reflexes in their hands and then I had them take off their shoes and showed them certain reflexes in their feet. They loved it. That was one month ago; I wish you could see the difference in my people now. Many of them are much healthier and in brighter spirits. Every day someone comes to tell me of the wonderful results they are having since I showed them the miracle of massaging the reflexes.

Reflexology is truly a miracle from God that we have had with us all the time.

We pray for you every day, we thank God and we thank you for the miracle of reflexology.

—Rev. D. W.

2

How to Use Certain Exercises
to Stimulate the Reflexes on the Head

Several diagrams of the head are included in this chapter. As you study them, you will be amazed at the many reflexes you will find and how they are related to all parts of your body.

When I give you specific directions on how to stimulate the reflexes, you will better understand their importance. You need not learn where all these reflexes are located by sight, but with a little practice you will learn their approximate locations by feel. This will hold true in most cases throughout this book. Study the diagrams and photos as we progress.

TECHNIQUE FOR MASSAGING THE REFLEXES IN THE HEAD

Study Diagrams 2, 3, and 4. Take note of how many important reflexes are located here. You need not remember where they are located; I will point these out to you as we need them further on in the book. I just want you to familiarize yourself with the importance of the different techniques of massaging the reflexes in the head.

Use your fingers to find special areas on the head. In Diagram 2, notice on the very center of the top of the head we find the reflexes to the reproductive organs. Down toward the nose is the reflex to the pineal. Under the nose we find the reflex to the pineal and pituitary, then the spleen and the pancreas reflexes. Straight down from these reflexes we find the gonad reflexes on the chin. This seems to be on the center meridian line that runs through the body.

One way to massage these reflexes is to use the center finger, which is called the fire finger because it sends out energy more strongly than the other fingers. Press it on the center of the forehead just below the hair line. With a pressing, rolling motion feel for a

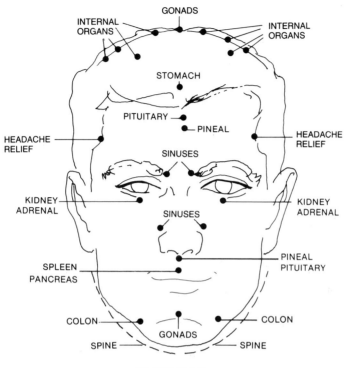

GONADS

INTERNAL ORGANS

INTERNAL ORGANS

STOMACH

PITUITARY

PINEAL

HEADACHE RELIEF

HEADACHE RELIEF

SINUSES

KIDNEY ADRENAL

KIDNEY ADRENAL

SINUSES

PINEAL PITUITARY

SPLEEN PANCREAS

COLON

COLON

GONADS

SPINE

SPINE

DIAGRAM 2

sensitive spot. You do not rub the skin, you rub the bone area under the skin very gently. Now, move the finger down to the center of the forehead and feel for another tender button, which will be a reflex to the pineal, (commonly known as the third eye). Halfway between this spot and the bridge of the nose is another sensitive reflex which needs massage. This affects the sinuses.

Massaging Only Certain Reflexes

This is one way to massage specific reflex buttons on the head. But you do not need to massage each and every one of these reflexes unless told to do so for a specific purpose later in the book. Other and easier methods of stimulating all of these head and face reflexes more fully will be described later. But, for now, do note that head massages are very important.

Look at Diagram 3, illustrating the back of the head. Notice all the reflexes located here. Now go to Diagram 4 to see the location of the reflexes on the side of the head. You may have to refer back to these charts now and then when following directions for treating malfunc-

Back of the Head

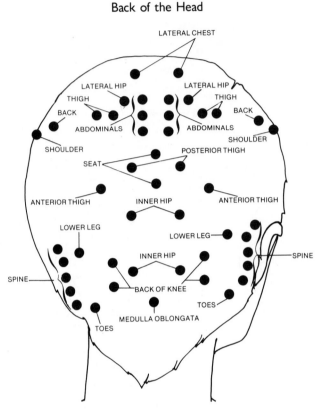

DIAGRAM 3

tioning areas elsewhere in the body. We will use three different methods of stimulation.

Methods of Stimulation

1. Grab handfuls of hair and pull. This not only stimulates the hair, but also the reflexes to the whole body. See Photo 1.
2. Close your fists very loosely and swing them loosely from the wrists as if they were on hinges. Very gently use these loose fists to tap the head. See Photo 2. Tap it all over very quickly. Do not do this for more than thirty seconds. This will be enough to bring life to every organ and gland in your body.
3. If you have a wire brush, use this to tap the head gently all over. See Photo 3. This is an excellent reflex stimulator and also stimulates the hair follicles to help promote a new and luxurious head of hair.

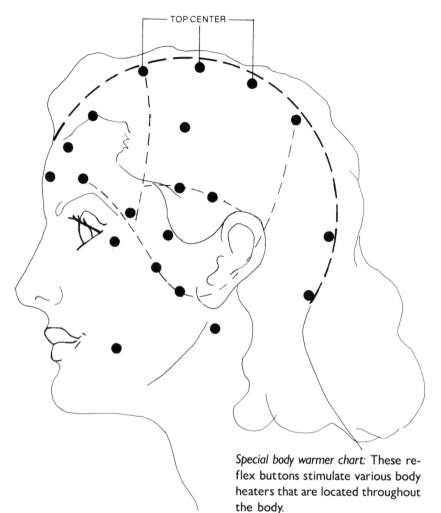

TOP CENTER

Special body warmer chart: These reflex buttons stimulate various body heaters that are located throughout the body.

DIAGRAM 4

ADJUSTMENT OF THE SKULL

The flow of cerebrospinal fluid is believed to be affected by the almost microscopic movement of the cranial bones during breathing. If these bones in the skull become stuck together it is thought that the fluid will not be pumped well enough through the spinal column; the muscles will weaken because the energy related to the cerebrospinal fluid cannot flow freely.

Adjustment of the cranial bones should be left to a doctor who is familiar with this technique. But if you find that the abdominal muscles are weak, this may be due to the parietal bones being jammed together at the top of the head. To strengthen the abdominal muscles you should massage the forehead as if to pull the skull apart along the seam. See Photo 4.

A car door once slammed on my head; it was caught between the top of the car and the door. I felt funny and had odd headaches for several days. I felt that the cranial bones had been jammed together. No doctors in the area were familiar with this method of treatment, so I started to press and pull the cranial bones myself. After a few days I felt better and the uncomfortable sensations in my head stopped. This was several years ago, and I still feel fine.

THE ALL-IMPORTANT MEDULLA OBLONGATA

The medulla oblongata is a reflex button that we will use throughout this book. It is one of the magic buttons that will start your power generator into action. It will enable you to open up the electrical channels to all parts of the body. It will bring you release from daily nervous tensions when you need it. This button will stimulate almost instant energy. You decide on the action you want and in seconds it is yours to command. This magic reflex button can be used at any time and in almost any location without anyone knowing what you are doing.

In Diagram 3 notice the button located in the hollow at the base of the skull on the back of the head. This is the medulla oblongata, a vitality-generating reflex button. It is the enlarged portion of the spinal cord, just after it enters the cranium. It is a giant controlling agent containing the cardiovascular center and the respiratory center. It controls blood pressure and the dilation and constriction of blood vessels. It controls postural balance and the reflexes concerned with swallowing, vomiting, and many other actions. Even though the spinal cord is located on the inside of the skull, you will cause reactions whenever you apply any type of reflex therapy to it. The entire body network funnels impulses into the spinal cord. These messages are relayed to the power-manufacturing centers of the brain and body. The messages are sent to all of the endocrine glands. We have just learned the importance of each one of these glands, how each gland is a producer of important hormones, and how each one of these glands is a source of health, beauty, vigor, and vitality.

The medulla oblongata reflex will give you instant go-power when it is needed. It is a very important reflex button and will be referred to many times in this book, so it is important that you learn the best technique for massaging it.

Technique of Reflex Massage

To turn on this sensational dynamo of action, find a little hollow between two muscle attachments at the base of the skull. See medulla oblongata, Diagram 3. Use either the middle finger of one hand or the middle fingers of both hands. You will have to use the method that is easiest for you. Now, put the finger or fingers into the hollow area and press. Is it painful? Feel it! Press it! Massage it! This is the fantastic magic reflex button that can give you the unlimited energy and go-power that everyone needs in these busy, stress-filled days.

SPECIAL BODY WARMER REFLEXES

As you study Diagram 4, you will see special points marked in various places on the side of the head. These are known as neuro-vascular receptors. I call them the body warmer reflexes to keep them simple and easy to remember. Each of these special reflexes are in relative positions. Remember that all heads are not the same shape, so you have to learn the approximate areas by searching for tender or sensitive points. With practice, you will learn to find them on yourself and others quite easily by reaching and feeling with your fingers. See Photos 4, 5, 6, 7, and 8 for different positions used to massage these body warmer reflexes on the head. These body warmer reflexes keep the lines open to special heaters in various parts of the body.

Let us liken the body warmers to little electric heaters that control the temperature of the entire body. If you are unable to adjust to temperature changes in the weather, some of your body heaters are not functioning properly and need to be reactivated.

These body warmers gather and regulate the energy of the digestive, sexual, and respiratory organs, and others. They work in cooperation with the lungs, the small intestines, the kidneys, the heart, and the sex organs.

The meridian of the body warmers begins at the root of the nail of the little finger and ascends up the back part of the body. If you will look once more at Diagram 4, you will better understand how the exercises that I give you to massage the head will help stimulate most, if not all, of the body warmer reflexes in the whole body.

As we massage the reflexes in other places of the body, we automatically press on and massage many of the body warmers without having to learn their exact locations. Keep in mind that if you find a tender reflex, no matter what part of the body it is getting a distress signal from, you should press and hold it until the hurt subsides.

3

Techniques for Massaging Reflexes All Over the Body

In describing how to use reflexes found all over the body, it is best to start with those found in the hands and feet.

Place your thumb in the center of your palm or in the center of the bottom of your foot and, with a rotating motion, press and roll the thumb as if you were trying to break up lumpy sugar. Do this about five times, then move to another spot. You can tell which reflex you are massaging by studying Diagrams 5, 6, 7, and 8. You are *not* to rub the skin but the reflexes under the skin. Use this method for massaging reflexes, except where instructed to hold a steady pressure.

A more advanced method of massaging the hands and the feet involves starting to rub the thumb or the big toe, then completely massaging every finger and every toe, searching for tender reflexes. Don't just use your fingers here. Use a device like a pencil or the little hand reflex probe described in the chapter on reflex devices. Roll this between every toe on both sides and also between every finger. You will be amazed at the "ouch" spots you will discover in these areas.

In Diagrams 9A, 9D, and 9E, you will find that there are also important reflexes on the tops of the feet and on the backs of the hands. Be sure to massage these reflex buttons to stimulate many areas in the body. Hold a steady, firm pressure for a slow count of seven, then release for a count of three. Do this three times more if you think it necessary. For the reflexes designated "pain," use the fingers of the left hand and hold for several minutes. Hold the hands on the calves of the legs for about fifteen minutes to alleviate pain throughout the entire body. See Diagram 9H.

ENDOCRINE GLAND REFLEX POINTS

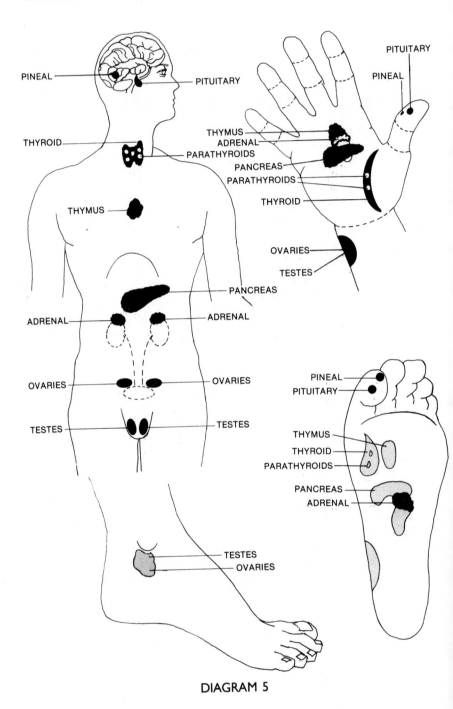

DIAGRAM 5

REFLEX HAND CHART

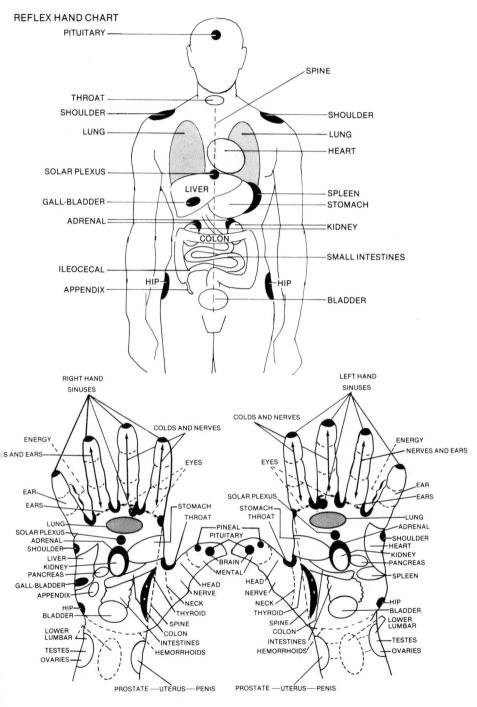

DIAGRAM 6

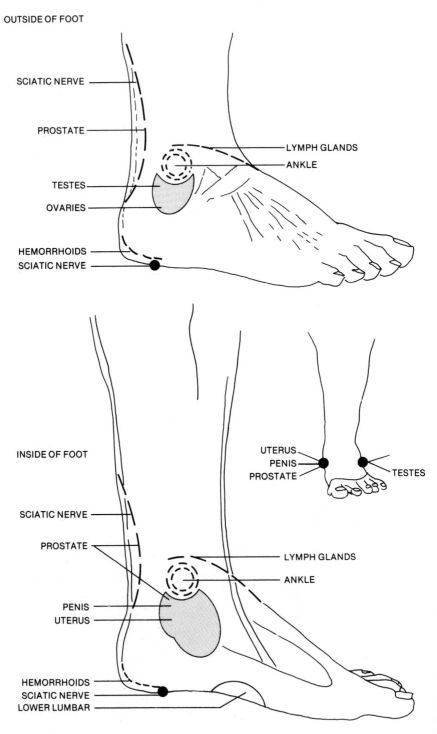

DIAGRAM 7

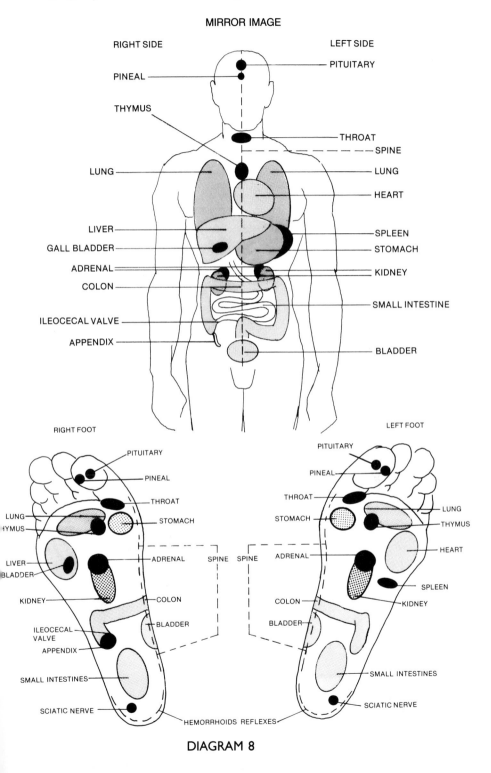

DIAGRAM 8

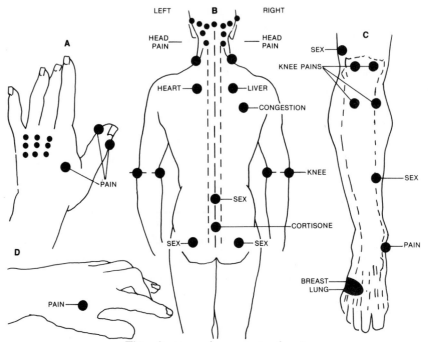

This diagram shows several pain control reflex buttons that are stimulated by pressure that causes them to release natural pain-inhibiting chemicals in the brain called "endorphines." Also shown are energy-stimulating reflex buttons in various locations.

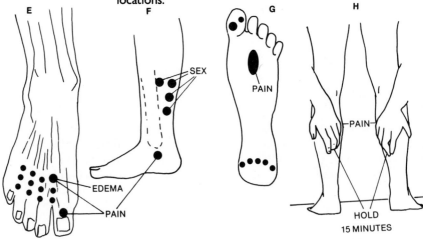

DIAGRAM 9

The Electrical Power in Your Hands

The palm of the right hand is positive and stimulates energy, which has a strengthening effect.

The palm of the left hand is negative and has a sedating, soothing, and cleaning effect.

The use of both hands will give you the combined effect of both energies.

The backs of the hands have the opposite electrical energy from the palms. The back of the right hand will be negative and the back of the left hand will be positive.

The back of the head is positive while the front of the head is negative. If you place the palm of your right hand on the lower part of the back of your head and place the palm of the left hand on the front part of the head, you will be enforcing the natural energies of the head, and a feeling of well-being and strength will be the result. If you reverse this procedure, you will have a lowering of the efficiency of the brain which will have a disturbing effect.

So remember, when you are pressing a reflex button to stop pain, try to use the left hand. If you are using a reflex implement for pain, hold it in your left hand. If you are seeking to send the energized healing forces to slow, stagnated, and clogged areas in the body, you may gain better results by using the strengthening effect of the right hand.

Reflexology is a natural method of healing, no matter where or how it is used, but it might give more confidence to some who feel that their healing is not progressing as fast as they would like if they are aware of the positive and negative electrical power in their hands. God heals what doctors can't! Reflexology is *one* of his many gifts to natural health, *and it is free!*

A Husband's Life Is Prolonged

Dear Mrs. Carter,

The doctors said my husband would not live a week. After talking to you I started to give him reflexology on his whole body. I had your books on foot and hand reflexology, which helped keep him alive. Then I advanced to body reflexology and he lived for four more years. The doctors think I am crazy to use reflexology, but it did for him what they could not do, and I am still alive and healthy today thanks to reflexology.

I thank you for your help and God bless you in your wonderful work for humanity.

—M. L.

BODY REFLEXES

You can see by studying the diagrams that follow that, unlike the reflexes in the hands and the feet, body reflexes do not always follow a straight meridian line. There are *several* reflex points located in certain areas of the body that will stimulate renewed life to more than one malfunctioning area.

So, we will have to use a somewhat new technique when using the body reflexes. Because these reflex buttons are sometimes in hard-to-massage areas, it is difficult to give simple directions.

By studying the diagrams, you will see what I mean. In Diagram 2, notice how many reflexes are located in just a portion of the head. How are you going to find a specific button? Hence some new techniques come into play. You will find photos of most of them. Sometimes it may be necessary to ask another person for help.

Look at Diagrams 10 and 11. You will see reflex points scattered over various parts of the body. Now turn to Diagrams 12, 13, and 14. Many of you are not familiar with the glands and organs within the body; I would like you to study the positions of these glands and organs so you will be able to associate them with certain reflex buttons when you are instructed to massage them for specific ailments.

HOW TO MASSAGE BODY REFLEXES
FOR THE MOST EFFECTIVE RESULTS

Look at Diagrams 6 and 7. Note how the reflex buttons are located more or less over the glands and organs they represent. To massage these specific reflex points, use the middle finger, which has the strongest energy flow, or use the four-finger method, which sometimes seems to have the power of a laser beam. There are several ways in which you can massage these sensitive reflex buttons. All reflex buttons not named on the charts are energy stimulants and important to many areas of the body. You will find many tender reflex buttons that are not marked. Don't let this worry you. If they are sending an "ouch" signal, this means that some place in your body is in trouble and asking for your help. So massage it out.

It is best to start by massaging the *important* reflexes located in various places over the entire body.

Use the middle finger to press lightly on each reflex button. If it is painful, you will know that there is congestion somewhere. Let us say that you find a painful button over the stomach area. This does not

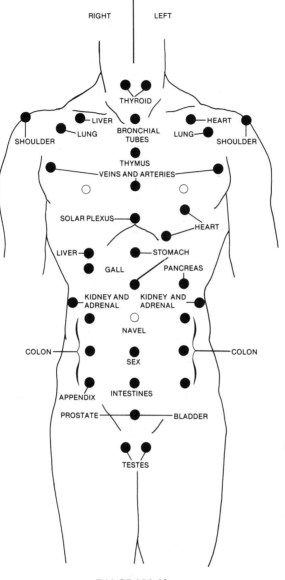

RIGHT | LEFT

THYROID

LIVER
LUNG
SHOULDER

BRONCHIAL
TUBES

HEART
LUNG
SHOULDER

THYMUS
VEINS AND ARTERIES

SOLAR PLEXUS

HEART

LIVER

STOMACH

GALL

PANCREAS

KIDNEY AND
ADRENAL

KIDNEY AND
ADRENAL

NAVEL

COLON

COLON

SEX

APPENDIX

INTESTINES

PROSTATE

BLADDER

TESTES

DIAGRAM 10

necessarily mean that the stomach is the organ in trouble. When you look at Diagrams 10 and 11, you can see that tender reflexes could be sending out pain signals from other malfunctioning nerves or tissue in a congested area. If it hurts when pressed, assume that there is a blocked line that is slowing down the electrical life force to a congested area. Hold pressure on this reflex button until the hurt

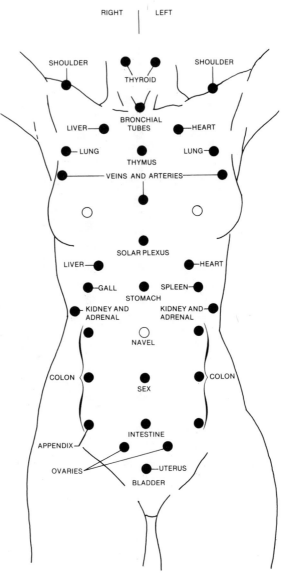

DIAGRAM II

subsides or for seven seconds at a time. Keep in mind that you are doing more than diagnosing areas of malfunction when you massage these reflexes that are giving you warning signals of congestion or malfunctioning of a certain organ, gland, or tissue. You are also treating the *ailment,* restoring health by releasing the blockage to the energy field.

MIRROR IMAGE

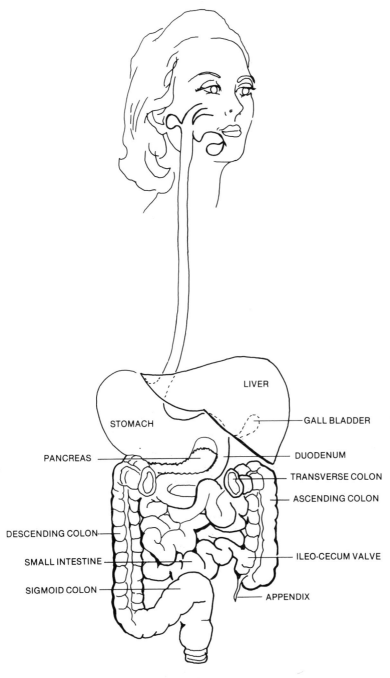

DIAGRAM 12

MIRROR IMAGE

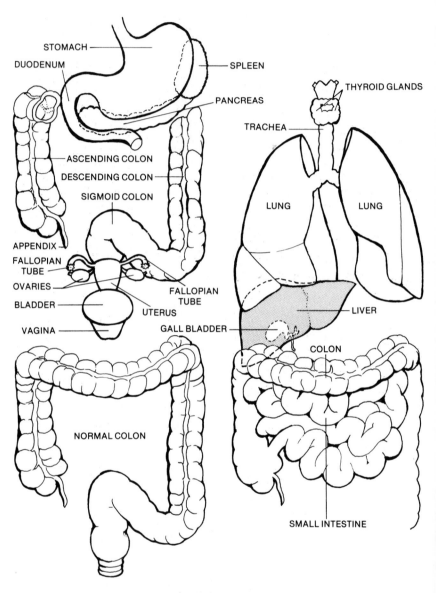

DIAGRAM 13

On the chest and abdomen, we will use finger pressure to massage the reflexes. See Photos 9, 10, 11, 12, and 13. However, some people like to use a device called the reflex roller in these areas. See Photos 14 and 15. I will explain how to use the reflex implements in a later chapter.

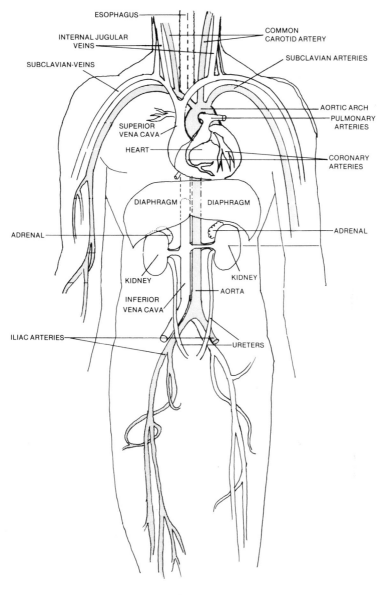

DIAGRAM 14

Body Reflexology Aids a Woman Who Lives Alone

Dear Mrs. Carter,

I want to thank you for telling me about reflexology. I am seventy-three years old and live by myself out in the country. I have always been very healthy so I don't mind living so far from people. Then I got to feeling bad, and it seemed that all at once my body didn't function well. I felt worse and worse every day, so

I decided to call you. I had used reflexology for many years to stay healthy. Now I needed to know what was wrong.

After you explained about body reflexology and told me how to use it along with the foot and hand massages, I have completely recovered and feel better than ever. My friends did talk me into going to a doctor after you told me I should. He said I was in perfect health, younger than my years, and he told me that whatever I was doing, to keep doing it.

I am so grateful to you. Thank you again, dear lady.

—M. G.

Using the Reflex Pulse Test on the Abdomen

With the middle finger, or using all fingers held together on one or both hands, press into your navel firmly but gently. To get the full benefit from this test, it will be best if you lie on your back. If you have a pad of fat over the abdominal area, then you will have to use the fingers to press in deeply through the fat pad. Now, feel for a pulse beat. Do you feel the pulse throb? If you do, this indicates that there is trouble in this area and it needs help. How do you give it help? Hold pressure on this reflex for the count of seven. Then use a slight rotary movement, keeping the fingers on the area of the pulse beat.

Now we will go to other reflex buttons in the abdomen. Look at Diagrams 10 and 11. Using this same test method with the finger, feel each indicated reflex button for the beat of the pulse. If you cannot find a pulse beat, you can be happy to know that this area is free from trouble. If you do feel the throb of the pulse, then you know that it means malfunctioning of the organ or trouble in the zone for this reflex point.

Remember to sedate all reflexes that are painful on light pressure by holding to the count of seven. If you have to press in deeply to feel the throb of the pulse, you should stimulate the point by using heavier pressure. Many of these reflexes may be quite painful when pressed. By pressing and massaging these "ouch" points, you will be amazed at how quickly the pain subsides. Usually this happens while you are using the reflex pressure system. It will really amaze you when you feel the pain disappear under your very fingertips. You will have performed a miracle of healing, for, when the pulse can no longer be felt and the pain under your fingers has subsided, it means that the problem in the corresponding organ also has subsided. You have released the healing forces of nature to revive glandular activity!

Morning Reflexology Test

Before you get up each morning take a reflexology test by pressing reflex buttons in the abdomen and the chest. This will not only be a test for danger signals but you will also give added stimulation to organs and glands to help prevent any congestion that might be accumulating along life lines to parts all over the body.

When the pain stops at the point of finger pressure, you will know that tension has been released and you will also feel that the pain coming from another part of the body has subsided. When you arise, you will have a feeling of energy and well-being that you have not felt for a long time.

I want you to do these exercises every morning, not only to *put* you in good health but also to *keep* you feeling full of energy and perfect health for the rest of your long life.

If you can feel the pulse or a hurt in a certain reflex spot, use a rotary motion with the finger for a few seconds to help dissipate the painful reflex button.

Now, we will assume that you are lying down on your back with your abdomen exposed. Place your middle finger in your navel and feel for a pulse beat. See Photo 10. After holding this for the count of seven, massage around the navel using all of the fingers except the thumb. Now with the palm of the hand start massaging at the navel in a clockwise motion, working outward in an ever larger circle until you are massaging the whole abdomen. Do this three times, then repeat counterclockwise. You can see how the energy of your hand will stimulate the entire abdominal area. Remember, when pain radiates from the navel to other parts of the body, the massage is not only a test but also a treatment for ailing parts of the body.

The Ice Cube Technique

When massaging any of the reflex buttons that seem to resist full recovery, you might try using the ice cube method. Use the same rotary motion on the tender reflex button with the corner of an ice cube. Press it on the sore button for about three seconds, then lay the hand on the spot for a second, then repeat with the ice cube once more.

Reflexes on the Chest

Now, proceed to the reflex points on the chest. See Photos 9, 13, and 14. Use the same massage on these reflex buttons as you did on the abdomen, except you will find that these reflex buttons will be located mostly over bone and muscle so that you will not press the fingers in as deeply as you did on the abdomen. You will still hold a steady pressure to test for tender spots, using the rotating massage when you find an "ouch" button. In many cases, tapping several times with the fingers will give better results. Although many points pictured on the charts are special reflex buttons for specific glands and organs, feel for added reflex points as you cover the chest and abdomen with your fingertips. Many people like to use the reflex roller to help them locate tender reflexes that they might have overlooked when using only the fingers. (See Photos 14 and 15.)

A Boost of Electrical Energy

Now, before you get out of bed, buff your nails to give yourself a boost of electrical energy that will fill your whole being with an electrical radiance and will last you all day. (See Photo 16.) In my book, *Hand Reflexology: Key to Perfect Health*, I told how to buff the nails to stimulate the growth of new hair. Since then, I have had many reports of how it also stimulates renewed electrical energy and vitality to the whole body.

You will find a fuller explanation of how to buff the nails in the chapter on hair.

4

How to Use Reflexology on the Ears

Let us move on to Diagram 15, which involves the ears. There are many important reflexes in the ears. They will stimulate a renewed flow of life force into every part of your body when pressed, pulled, and massaged. The ears, like the hands and the feet, have reflexes for the entire body.

In recent generations, people's ears have become atrophied and shriveled. Yet, they are an extension and reflection of all of the body's organs and their condition. Take the earlobe, for instance. It gives us an accurate report on your biological strength, happiness, and fortune. These qualities are shown in fleshy, long, hanging earlobes, well separated from the cheek. All great men, including tycoons, millionaires, and great philosophers, exhibited these large earlobes. Today, many of the frantic breed of tycoons have stunted, creased, gnarled earlobes clinging tightly to their cheeks. This shows malfunction of the organs elsewhere in the body. The mental and physical condition of the individual is very accurately shown by the balance of the ear form.

Because of the relationship of the reflexes in the ears to the rest of the body, reflex massage of the ears can be of help in correcting many symptoms of malfunctioning organs.

Remember when you were a child, and a teacher or an angry adult grabbed you by the ear and dragged you off for punishment? It is now known that your reflexes were being stimulated (effectively correcting an organic condition), and this was responsible for restoring natural function. Another restorative massage that we now recognize, but which was very unpleasant at the time, was the vigorous scrubbing behind the ears with lots of cold water. This was a healthy stimulant to many areas in the rest of the body. In the past, our forefathers had to rely on instinct in almost everything they did— or were they aware of the actual good health fostered by some of the

THE EAR

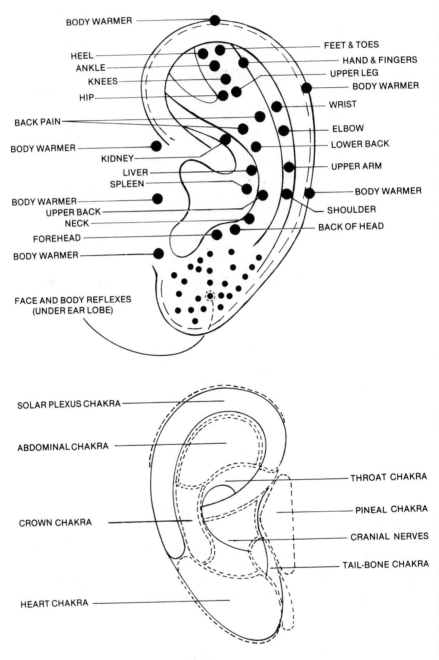

DIAGRAM 15

punishments they meted out to the younger generation? They produced health besides building respect and making responsible, happy, trustworthy adults in later life.

We can see how tapping on the head with a thimble stimulated reflexes to several areas in the body, according to where the thimble landed. See Diagrams 2, 3, and 4. I think that being tapped on the head by a thimble-wielding aunt was the biggest insult to my dignity. But it certainly got my adrenalin flowing. Notice in Diagram 2 that the adrenal reflexes are near the top of your head.

I wonder if there are special reflexes that got stimulated on the bottom when we were "tanned" there as children? Maybe one reason we have so much delinquency among our younger generation today is that their body reflexes need more frequent stimulation. I never got many spankings, but I felt that I needed every one I got, and I held no anger toward my parents because of them. It is unjust punishment that children and adults resent.

Let me tell you the story of a farmer who raised fruit trees and used to hire a little boy every spring to go out into the orchard and whip the trees. Yes! He had a stick with many wires fastened to it and the boy had to whip every tree all the way around with this wire whip. I don't know if this really did any good, but I do know that he had the healthiest trees and the largest, juiciest fruit in the country.

You can see by looking at some of the diagrams in later chapters that when we were whipped on the legs or on the bottom branches of reflexes were stimulated.

Does "spare the rod and spoil the child" have a new meaning?

THE EAR AND ITS ACUPOINTS

Now, let us return to the ear, which is a complex sense organ endowed with a hundred acupoints. Its accessibility makes it ideal for the acupuncturist, who uses needles for stimulation to promote health in the rest of the body.

We have now learned to use the fingers to stimulate these sensitive reflexes. People twist, pull, and pinch their ears unconsciously, especially the earlobes, when something perplexing bothers them. Thus, instinctively, people reinvent this wonderful healing technique.

Because there are some 100 reflexes in the ears, it is almost impossible to pinpoint all of them, so let us do a few exercises to stimulate as many of them as possible.

See Photo 17. Place the fingers behind the ears and flatten them forward against the side of the head. Holding the ear with the third, fourth, and fifth fingers, tap the index finger on the ear to get a drum sound. Do this about five times to stimulate the gall bladder.

Now, place the cupped hand over one ear and tap gently with the other hand to get the sound of a seashell. This stimulates the kidneys and the triple-warmer organs.

Diagnosing Illness by Examining the Ears

Medical researchers tell us that the ear can be used to diagnose pain and illness in the rest of the body by observing temperature change and tenderness. Accuracy in ear diagnosis is said to be so good that an expert can achieve up to 90 percent accuracy in diagnosis of many conditions.

There are various changes in certain parts of the ear when specific areas of the body are stimulated. The ear can become very painful to the touch in a localized area corresponding to a specific part of the body.

Reflex pressure used on specific areas of the ear has been demonstrated on the stage, where almost immediate results were accomplished. The subjects who were worked on recovered from various illnesses almost immediately.

You may be able to find relief for malfunctioning areas in other parts of the body by using reflex pressure on specific buttons on the ear. See Diagram 15. Since the ear is such a small area to contain so many reflexes, you will have to use the press-and-feel technique. You might press with the fingernails or use reflex clamps. See Photos 18, 19, and 20.

Follow our motto, "If it is sore, rub it out," even if you don't know exactly what part of the body it corresponds to. If a certain point in the ear is painful to the touch, it means there is a health problem in some other area of the body that is sending a call for help. Somewhere a line is not getting its full supply of energy. By pressing the tender reflex in the ear, you are contacting another main circuit that will open up the line to full power. Remember to check the ear reflexes along with all other reflex points when you have health problems to overcome.

STIMULATING REFLEXES ON THE EARS

Starting at the tops of the ears, pinch them between the thumbs and forefingers. Doing both ears at the same time, pinch this whole area using a pinch-and-roll technique. See Photo 19. You will probably find many tender reflexes as you progress along the entire ear. Tug the ears upward, keeping them close to the head. Lower your fingers to the narrow part of the ears, still using the pinch-and-roll method, and pull the ears out away from the head. Do this several times. Notice how they begin to tingle and burn.

Let us progress down to the lower lobes of the ears. Use the pinch-and-roll method of massage to pull, tug, and pinch these lobes for a few seconds. See Photo 20. Then, with the fingers, start at the top of the ear and pinch and roll the outer ridge all the way around to the lobes. Now hook the little fingers in the holes of the ears and pull out in all directions. End this massage by pinching and massaging the small flap (the tragus) located in front of the ear opening.

Now press the reflex buttons just behind the lobes of the ears, first on the bony section, then in the hollow. These also are magic reflex buttons that can free you from tension and cure sinus problems and headaches.

HOW TO HELP TINNITUS

Tinnitus is an upsetting problem caused by strange noises in the ears or the head. In some cases, it has been thought impossible to cure, but I believe that any kind of distress can be cured by nature. First, make sure there is no buildup of wax in the ear. See Diagram 15 and massage all of the ear reflexes, giving special attention to reflexes labeled as body warmers and the reflex located under the earlobe. There are three body warmer reflexes for each ear in addition to the reflex on the hollow under the earlobes. Do both ears by pinching, rolling, and squeezing each reflex for the slow count of seven. See Photos 19 and 20.

Scuba Diver's Ears Helped by Reflexology

While waiting for a chartered boat in Hawaii, I started talking with a young girl sitting next to me in a coffee shop.

She told me that she taught deep sea and scuba diving, though she seemed young for that kind of work. She told me that her ears had become "scratched." (That is the term they use when the ear has been damaged from diving too deeply or coming to the surface too quickly).

The inside of her head itched, so it nearly drove her mad sometimes, and she was told nothing could be done for it. I am always interested in learning what reflexology will do in unusual cases like this, so I asked her to let me have her hand for a moment. Because only the right ear was affected, I took her right hand and found the ring finger and the little finger to be tender. I massaged them a few seconds; you wouldn't believe the strange look that came into her eyes. She said, "It's stopped itching! I can't believe it. My head feels clear and normal. What did you do?"

I showed her where and how to massage the reflexes to the ears and told her to teach it to her diving companions to prevent such problems in the future. I also told her to do the same with her toes to help overcome what might be even more serious complaints caused by deep diving.

THE REFLEX BUTTONS THAT HELP HEARING

It may not seem possible that by pressing a few reflexes a person who has been unable to hear for many years can suddenly regain his or her hearing. To these people, it is truly a very wonderful miracle.

Physicians familiar with the practice of reflexology have used this method for years to help the deaf hear. Osteopaths, chiropractors, and naturopathic doctors who have used this method of healing have had some very startling results.

Curing Deafness

In a previous book I told of many people who regained their hearing, some having been deaf for years. You, too, can use this simple method of reflexology to restore hearing to the deaf.

One of the simple methods that they used to bring back their hearing was to press the end of the fourth finger, the ring finger, for several minutes at a time, doing this several times a day when possible. This will also relieve an earache in most cases.

The Hard-Cotton Method

The hard-cotton method has been used successfully by many doctors. You can use any sterile object, such as a hard eraser or whatever object will serve you best. Place this object in the space between the last tooth and the jaw, in back of the wisdom tooth. You will be pressing on a reflex button that goes to the ear and is stimulated by a steady pressure. Bite down on this object for about five minutes at a time. Repeat this treatment several times a day.

The reflex comb is also very helpful in stimulating the ears. Press the teeth of the comb to the tips of all of the fingers and hold the pressure for about five minutes. See Photo 21.

Reflexology for Hearing

One of my students told me of a man who came to her who was almost deaf. He could not hear very well even with a hearing aid. Without the hearing aid, he could hear practically nothing. After three or four visits to her for reflexology treatments, his hearing was greatly improved. She said the other day he told her that he could even hear the water running in a little creek that runs by his home, something he had never heard before. His hearing gets better every day and he has thrown away his hearing aid.

Dear Mrs. Carter,
    Just found out firsthand about reflexology and it worked for me. I couldn't hear correctly for more than forty years because my left ear was damaged during the war. Using reflex clamps on my left finger twice a day did the trick, and now I can even hear my wristwatch tick clearly.

                             —Reverend S. H.

5

How to Use Reflex Massage on the Tongue

The mouth and the tongue are not given enough consideration in most discussions of the healing forces of the body. All of the food that we eat and all of the liquids that we drink pass into the mouth and over the tongue. Many intricate, sensitive cells are exposed to all of the elements as we drink hot and cold liquids. Alcoholic beverages and good foods and bad have to pass through this channel before we can nourish our bodies. Think of the importance of this organ as you study and learn to use the reflexes in the tongue and the mouth.

THE IMPORTANCE OF THE REFLEXES IN THE TONGUE

Most people don't realize that there are some very important reflexes in the mouth and the tongue. In fact, the tongue has reflex points that cover almost every part of the body. Everyone should have a tongue depressor and should use it every day to help keep in top condition. To prove this statement, take a tongue depressor or the handle of a spoon and press it on the tongue. See Photo 22. Turn it from side to side and press down. Feel the tender spots in various places on the tongue? By pressing the reflexes in the tongue you can overcome many types of pain and distress. Ten zones are in the tongue and they follow the pattern of the zones throughout the body. Note the zones in Diagram 16.

The reflexes in the center of the tongue correspond to the center of the body. So, as you press and stimulate the reflexes in the center of the tongue, you are sending the vital life force surging into all of the glands, organs, and cells that are located in the center of the body. As you press on the reflexes on the right side of the tongue, you are stimulating glands and organs on the right side of the body. And when you press the reflexes on the left side of the tongue you are

52

ZONE THERAPY

EACH NUMBERED LINE
REPRESENTS THE CENTER
OF ITS RESPECTIVE ZONE
ON THE BODY.

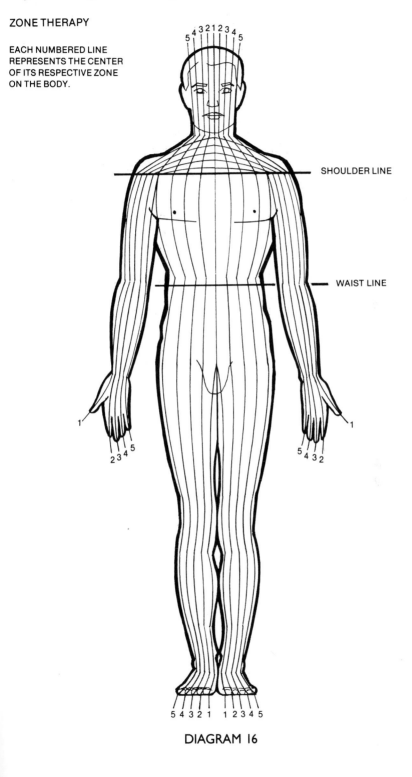

SHOULDER LINE

WAIST LINE

DIAGRAM 16

stimulating all of the glands and organs on the left side of the body. When you find an extremely tender spot in a certain area of the tongue, check the zone chart to find just where there is malfunction in the body. Then press and hold this tender spot for a count of seven.

CHECKING CORRESPONDING REFLEXES

Now, check the chart for other reflexes elsewhere on the body along this line, and when you press the ones corresponding to the reflex in the tongue you will find that they are very tender also. Massage any button that shows a slight bit of tenderness. Remember that when there is tenderness in any part of the body it is like a doorbell ringing to give you a message. The roller reflex massager is very helpful in locating tender buttons in various places on the body. This is explained more thoroughly in the chapter on reflex devices.

Many people claim that they are never without their tongue depressor; they carry it with them in a sanitary plastic bag wherever they go.

The tongue reflexes are used to stop the pain of menstruation for women almost immediately. A pregnant woman should not press tongue reflexes since this seems to have a relaxing effect on the reproductive organs and might cause a miscarriage. Since it does relax and stop pain in various parts of the body, the tongue reflex might also prove beneficial to men who suffer from prostate trouble. I have no evidence on this, but always remember that wherever there is distress in any part of the body, reflexology can help, never harm.

There are also other reflexes in the mouth that help distressed parts of the body. Reflex buttons under the tongue and on the roof of the mouth bring relief from many ailments. By pressing the top of the mouth with a clean thumb, you will be able to stop coughs in a few minutes, if nothing else helps.

THE VALUE OF TONGUE PULLING

Grasping the tongue with a clean tissue or cloth and pulling out as far as possible (while holding the tongue up slightly to prevent cutting the under side of the tongue on the teeth) has several benefits. It can cure a sick voice and stop hiccups. Some life-saving clinics teach that pulling out the tongue relieves a choking person.

TONGUE BRUSHING

Do you realize how important it really is to clean the tongue? The Orientals have relied on tongue cleaning for centuries. It was a routine practice for the ancient Romans and is still used in the Orient.

Sylvia, a Chinese woman who was my second mother, taught me the importance of cleaning the tongue many years ago. She insisted that the tongue be scraped at least every morning and every night before retiring. This was more important to her than brushing the teeth. I forget what we used to scrape our tongues with at that time, but the habit has stayed with me and I have always brushed my tongue clean when I brush my teeth. Maybe that is why I have never had problems with my teeth.

Sylvia taught me how the Orientals have used tongue scraping as a natural method for freshening the breath, protecting the teeth, and she also claimed many health benefits that I do not now remember, just by the simple method of keeping the deposits from the tongue and reducing the plaque-forming bacteria that lead to tooth decay.

The surface of the tongue is a breeding ground for bacteria. This germ-laden coating is a primary source of bad breath. Evidence has also been documented that plaque-forming streptococci counts increased ten times after a week of not cleaning the tongue.

The American Dental Association now encourages tongue cleaning. It has approved a tongue cleaner that is sold here in the United States called the Lila Tongue Cleaner. See Photo 23. If you are unable to find it on the market, you can purchase it from Stirling Enterprises, Cottage Grove, Oregon 97424.

6

How Teeth Can Be Helped with Reflexology

I know of no pain more unbearable than a toothache. I am lucky to have had very few problems with my teeth. The ones that I have suffered from have been caused by dentists. I had been exposed to severe cold and had gotton neuralgia in the nerves in my face, which was very painful. I thought that the pain might be caused by a tooth, but I couldn't get to see a dentist for several days. I knew that reflexology could help stop the pain, so I used clamps on my fingers off and on until I could see the dentist. This deadened the pain, and I don't know what made me keep my appointment with the dentist, but I did. When I got into the chair, he could not find anything wrong with my teeth. He was very concerned for my comfort, so he decided that he should pull one of my teeth even though the X-ray showed it to be perfect, as were all my teeth. I don't know why, but I let him pull it. I think that when we get in front of a doctor or a dentist we become hypnotized in some way. That is the only tooth that I have ever lost.

AN EFFECTIVE TOOTHPASTE

A dentist I went to many years ago for a mouth infection told me that I had perfect teeth and gums and asked what I used for toothpaste. I told him that I had used salt and soda all my life. He said that was the reason that I had hard, healthy gums and teeth. The glycerine used in toothpastes, he said, tended to soften the gums. When I mentioned this to certain other dentists, they made fun of me and said that it had nothing to do with my hard gums and perfect teeth.

Now we are told by Dr. Paul Keyes, clinical investigator at the National Institute of Dental Research, that gum disease can be prevented simply by brushing with *salt*. He says that if you have high blood pressure and are not supposed to use table salt, you can substitute Epsom salt.

HOW I MAKE MY TOOTH CLEANER

I use a salt shaker with large holes. In this, I put equal parts of salt and soda and two or three beans to keep the mixture from caking into hard lumps. I sprinkle a small amount of this in my hand and apply it with a dampened tooth brush. You will never have a fresher-feeling mouth or whiter teeth. The salt cleans and hardens the gums and the soda polishes the teeth "harmlessly." My children had perfect teeth until they left home and turned to the use of toothpastes and the consumption of sugared products such as candies and soft drinks. Maybe if they had kept using the salt and soda, the sugared products would have been less harmful to their teeth.

Dr. Keyes stresses that this program would be very beneficial for anyone with incipient pyorrhea. About 95 percent of the population suffers from some form of gum disease, from simple to advanced.

If you want fewer tooth problems, try the methods that I have described in this book. They will work wonders for you.

STOPPING A TOOTHACHE

To stop the pain of toothache, clamp down near the ends of the fingers. Check the meridian lines and press the fingers of the hand that is on the same side as the sore tooth. See Diagram 16. Follow the line that would go through the aching tooth down to the fingers on this same line, and put pressure on the fingers to which this line leads. This will anesthetize this area, and you will be free from pain. If you do not have clamps or rubber bands, hold pressure on the fingers with the teeth until the pain subsides. You will probably have to do this every fifteen to twenty minutes to keep the area deadened and free from pain until you can see a dentist.

Toothache Stopped with a Device

At a dinner dance one evening, the hostess told me she had an intolerable toothache. Since she had been a patient of mine, she was hoping I could help her. We went to the dressing room and I asked her for a comb. Since the tooth that was aching was on the left side, I began pressing her fingers on the left hand. I found some very tender spots on the inside of the thumb and index finger. Commencing with light pressure on these sensitive areas, I gradually increased the pressure on the comb while we talked of subjects pertaining to the party for about ten minutes. I asked how her tooth was, and she was astonished to find that the pain had left while we were talking. She enjoyed the rest of the evening without any further pain. I told her that she would be wise to use clamps on her fingers once in a while (and also a comb) until she could see her dentist. She ordered some clamps and a comb the next morning. She said that she would never be without them again.

An Embarrassing Situation Avoided

One evening, my husband was at a lodge meeting. A man sitting next to him complained of a terrible toothache and said he thought he would have to leave because of the pain. He was embarrassed as he was an important speaker for the evening. My husband told him to squeeze firmly on the joint of the middle finger, since the tooth that was causing him the pain was in the third meridian line of the body. The man knew that my husband was well informed on the healing methods of reflexology, so he followed the advice without any argument. He was amazed and very grateful to find that the tooth had completely stopped hurting by the time he was called on to give his talk. He told my husband later, when he thanked him for saving him from an embarrassing situation, that he was so amazed at the sudden relief from the toothache that he nearly forgot his speech.

Reflex Percussion of the Gums

Now let us reflex massage the buttons near the roots of the teeth. Press all of your fingers into your cheeks and feel for the roots of the upper teeth. Starting in front of the ears, work the fingers slowly toward the center of the face until you are pressing under the nose. Hold pressure on each of these buttons for about three seconds each. You may find some tender spots as your fingers travel over this area. When you do, hold pressure on this sore button a little longer, or go back and hold the pressure again later.

Now go to the roots of the lower teeth. Place all of the fingers along the line of the jawbone starting at the ears. As you press in, you will feel the roots of the lower teeth. Work your fingers along this area as you did on the roots of the upper teeth, pressing and massaging until you are working on the roots of the front teeth at the chin. See Photo 24. You stimulate the small and large intestine as well as the stomach meridians when you drum these areas with the fingers. While your fingers are in this position, place the thumbs under the chin and massage this area toward the chin. This helps reduce a double chin. See Photo 25.

A Test of Reflexology

A friend came to me one day suffering with a terrible toothache. We were in the mountains and there was no one to help her but me. She begged me to take her to a dentist, so I dropped everything and drove about twenty miles to a small country town where we found the dentist's office closed. We contacted the dentist and talked him into helping my friend, though he was against doing anything since she was pregnant and the tooth was ulcerated. He finally did pull the tooth after deadening it. When we were about halfway home, my friend started to cry and complained that she still had a toothache. I took her back to the dentist, but he refused to do anything for the other tooth, which was also badly abscessed. He told us that it would be too dangerous in her condition.

On the way home, I told her we would try reflexology on it. She was willing to try anything. As soon as we arrived home, I had her sit in a chair and give me her bare feet. I started to press on a big toe, and upon finding a very sore reflex on the top of the toe, I immediately used the press-and-massage method. In just seconds, she said, "Oh, it is getting better already." In about half an hour, the pain had completely subsided, and she went home promising to have her husband take her to a dentist as soon as he came home. We moved away soon after that, so I did not see her for several months. When I asked about her teeth, she said she hadn't gone to a dentist because the tooth had never bothered her again.

Don't forget to eat foods with plenty of calcium to nourish your teeth. A dentist tells of treating his patients with calcium and relieving them of all kinds of tooth diseases. The teeth actually healed themselves when nature was called in to do her work and was given the material to work with.

With a little knowledge about the tooth and its needs and how to give nature a helping hand, you may be able to keep your teeth for as long as you live.

7

How to Use Reflexology on the Eyes for Better Eyesight

Our eyes are truly a precious gift from God. Only those who have been denied the gift of sight or those who have lost it truly understand its importance.

Reflexology has helped many in different stages of blindness. It can do no harm and it is always of some benefit even if it fails to give a person perfect eyesight. Reflex massage always relaxes, no matter what one is using it for, and that in itself is good.

I hope that I can bring a new understanding to you who are having eye problems and that you will give reflex massage a good chance to prove to you that it really can help. You can also bring more beauty to the eyes by using reflex massage as directed.

MY TAPES FOR BLIND PEOPLE

I have made some tapes about reflexology at the request of the blind that I hope will bring as much help to them as my books have to those who can read. These tapes are not to enable the blind to regain their sight, but to help them understand and use reflex massage on their hands, feet, and other parts of their bodies to bring relief from pain and all type of illnesses, as it has to those of you who can read.

STIMULATING THE KIDNEYS

Two of the most important organs affecting the eyes are the kidneys.

To stimulate the kidneys, massage the reflexes in the center of the feet and also the hands. See Diagrams 6 and 8. See Diagrams 10 and

11 for body reflexes to the kidneys and work on these to help stimulate the eyes.

Now turn to the reflexes to the eyes themselves. In my previous books on foot reflexology and hand reflexology, I taught you to massage the reflexes just under the two toes next to the big toe where they fasten to the foot, doing this massage on both feet. Use the same massage on the two fingers next to the thumb. If these are tender, the reflexes are in need of massage to break loose certain blockages affecting the normal function of the eyes.

MASSAGING EYE REFLEXES FOR BETTER EYESIGHT

Now we turn to massage of the reflexes near the eyes for correction of many eye problems. The following method was worked out and used successfully by Therese Pfrimmer. If there is tightness of muscles around the eyes, they may pull on the eyeball, distort its shape, and cut off circulation, causing near- and far-sightedness. Tight eyelid muscles sometimes cause friction on the eyeball that can lead to the formation of cataract. If the eye muscles in the back of the eye are tight, the drainage ducts will be squeezed shut and won't empty properly. This can cause a buildup of fluid resulting in glaucoma.

To loosen the eye muscles, take your middle fingers and massage along the reflexes underneath both eyes. See Photo 26. Press in as you go across and feel for tight muscles. When you find that a muscle is tight, you will also probably find a hard spot or feel the muscles snap under your fingers. When you stimulate the reflexes to the eyes you immediately give renewed energy and life to your eyes. Don't do this very often at first. When you overstimulate the eyes, it can give you a terrible headache. I suggest that you do this only once the first day; then increase as you feel that you can, without any overstimulation. This holds true for the other eye reflex massages and also for the eye exercises I will give you later.

Move to the bones on top of the eyes and repeat the procedure. It may be easier to use the thumbs for this position. Work across the muscles and not with them when you do this massage.

Take your middle finger or thumb and work across the muscles on top of the nose starting deep in the eye socket. You will probably find this very tender, but remember our motto, "If it hurts, rub it out." Do this to both eyes; then go across the muscles on the forehead just above the eyebrows. If you feel a hard core or a tight band, you will know that you have found a tight muscle that may restrict the natural flow of electrical energy by way of the reflexes. It will probably be quite tender because the circulation of the vital life line is being blocked by these hard or tender areas.

Massaging these reflexes around the eyes can also help correct protruding eyes, eyes that hurt or are sensitive to light, and slanted eyes caused by muscle tension.

Massaging and tapping on the head can also help stimulate new life to the eyes. See the chapter on the head.

AN ALL-NATURAL EYE WASH

Another method of helping the eyes get back to normal is by using honey. Yes, you just put a drop or so of honey in the eyes and in a very short time you will notice an improvement in your eyes. It burns like fire at first, but only for a few seconds; the tears soon wash it out. I had a bad case of night blindness once. A lot of people were putting honey in their eyes, so I decided I would try it. A very short time after using honey, I was forced to drive home after dark. I had driven several miles when I realized that I could see just as well as I could in the daytime. That was several years ago, and I can still see well at night. I only used the honey about ten days, then got busy and forgot to use it again.

PALMING TO HELP THE EYES

Another thing that helps his eyes is to palm them. One man actually saved his eyesight by palming his eyes several times a day. To do this, put the palms of your hands on each eye, crossing the fingers over each other. Now, adjust them so that no light gets through. Keep your eyes open. Hold them in this position for a few minutes, being sure that you are looking into complete darkness. This is also very relaxing to the whole nervous system. Do it several times a day if you wish.

EYE EXERCISES

Now for some eye exercises, which are very helpful in strengthening the eyes. Years ago when my parents were prospecting in the Sierra Mountains, we met a doctor who taught us these exercises. I feel that because of them we didn't have to wear glasses for many years, and if we had kept up with the exercises we probably would never have had to wear them. I had my daughter do them after she got a bad eyestrain and went around blinking her eyes all the time. Her eyes returned to normal in just a few days.

Sit down where you can place a center mark on a wall directly in front of you, level with the eyes. A very tiny spot is all that is needed. I found that the bathroom was an excellent place for this since it only takes a few minutes and it is one place that you aren't disturbed. You might want to place a mark in each bathroom if you have a large family and teach them all how to use this eye-strengthening exercise. It can cut down on doctor bills.

You are now sitting with the spot directly in front of you. *Very slowly* turn your eyes to the left as far as you can without moving the head and *very slowly* bring them back to the center spot. Repeat the procedure looking to the right and back. From the center spot, lift the eyes up as far as possible and bring them down again to the spot and look down as far as possible. Be sure and keep the head straight and always bring the eyes back to the marked spot before doing the next movement. Do this only once the first few days. If you overdo these exercises, you will get one of the worst headaches you have ever had. This proves how very potent they are. Increase the number of repetitions every few days until you can do them ten times a day.

After the eyes have become used to this exercise, start to roll the eyes. Turn the eyes to the left as far as you can, then start to roll them up *slowly*. Roll them up and to the right, then down and on around till you have them back on the left side. Do this only once a day to start. Keep the head straight and do this exercise *very slowly*. You may gradually work this up to ten times a day.

How many times do you look a long distance away? Practice looking at great distances and then at something very close. These muscles need exercise, too.

You should be able to develop perfect eyesight by using one or several of the methods that I have given you.

Teach these eye-strengthening methods to your children, and they may be blessed with perfect eyesight the rest of their lives.

Using Clamps on the Eyebrows

Dear Mrs. Carter:

I have been experimenting with reflexology clamps and they truly work miracles on many parts of the body besides the fingers and toes. By placing them on the lips you can stimulate the circulation to the sagging muscles around the mouth. By putting them on the eyebrows they not only stimulate circulation to the wrinkles around the eyes but strengthen the eyes as well. When I showed these clamps to a doctor, he immediately put one on his eyebrow, instead of his finger, before I had time to tell him how to use them.

He is very enthusiastic about the possibilities of stimulating the healing life force in many parts of the body. He says by using this form of pressure on any part of the body it will increase the productivity of healing by added circulation.

—C. S.

Photo 1: Pulling hair stimulates the whole body, helps indigestion, hangovers, etc.

Photo 2: Lightly tapping head to promote bladder function and good sexual activity, as well as other benefits.

Photo 3: Tapping the
head and body with the
wire brush stimulates all
the body reflexes.

Photo 4: A position for massaging the reflexes in the head.

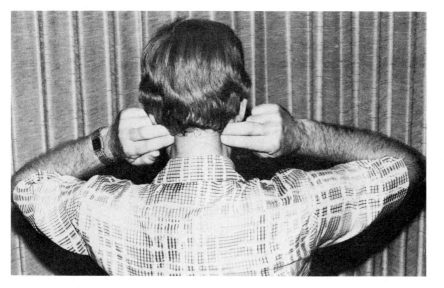

Photo 5: Pressing reflexes on the edge of the skull for headache and other complaints.

Photo 6: Position for massaging reflexes in the head to energize areas in the whole body.

Photo 7: Position for massaging reflexes in the head to energize many areas of the body.

Photo 8: Shows position for stimulating the thyroid, gonads, lungs, and heart.

Photo 9: Position for pressing reflexes to the thymus, veins, and arteries.

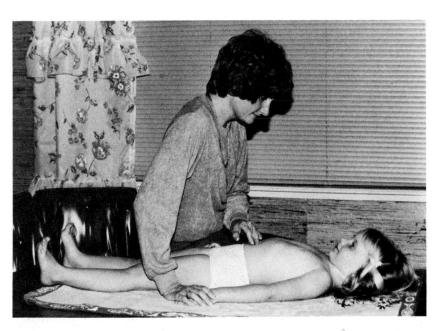

Photo 10: A light pressure on the stomach of a child to help an upset stomach, etc.

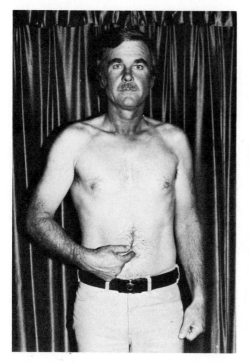

Photo 11: (left) Pressing finger into the navel to energize the whole body.

Photo 12: (below, left) Pressing finger on reflexes to stomach to relieve painful ulcers and other stomach problems.

Photo 13: (below) Pressing one of the reflex buttons for the heart.

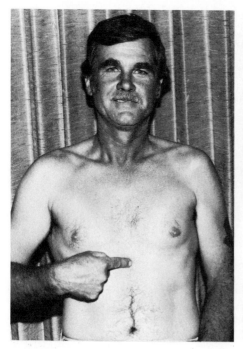

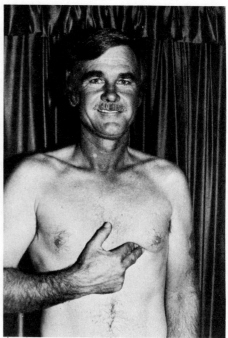

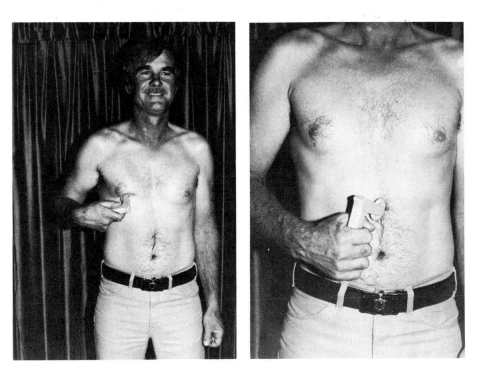

Photo 14: (above) How to use reflex roller to massage reflexes in the chest area.

Photo 15: (above, right) Using the reflex roller massager to stimulate abdominal reflexes.

Photo 16: (right) Position for buffing the nails to energize the whole body and promote the growth of hair.

Photo 17: Bending the ear forward for tapping.

Photo 18: Reflex clamp on the right ear to anesthetize areas on the right side of the body.

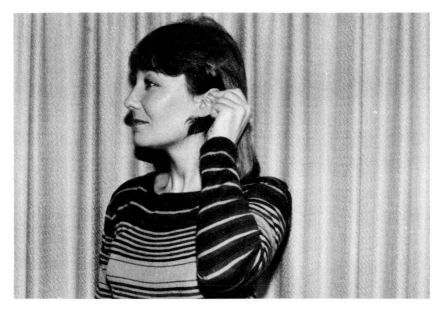

Photo 19: Massaging the reflexes in the ear for health and beauty.

Photo 20: Children can learn to massage the reflexes in their ears and other parts of the body with great benefit to their health.

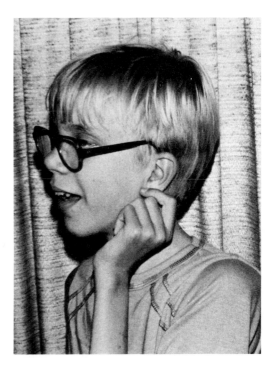

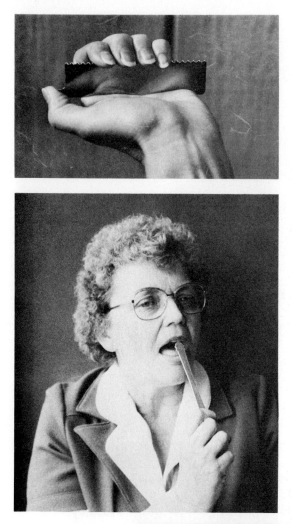

Photo 21: Position for holding reflex comb to alleviate pain in many parts of the body.

Photo 22: Shows reflex tongue probe ready to be used on the reflexes on the back of the tongue.

Photo 23: (below) How to use the tongue scraper to cleanse the tongue.

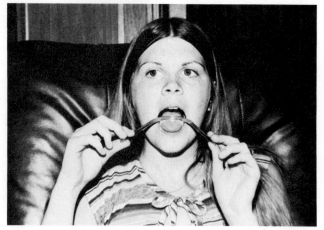

Photo 24: Position for pressing roots to lower teeth.

Photo 25: Pressing lymph nodes under the chin with the thumbs to make this area soft and pliable to increase energy and the flow of hormones for a better skin and fewer wrinkles.

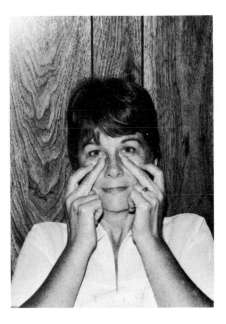

Photo 26: How to press the reflexes to the kidneys and adrenal glands for better eyesight.

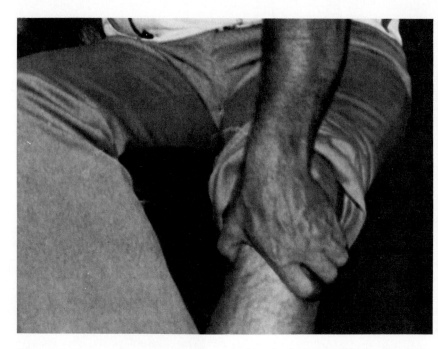

Photo 27: Position for pressing reflexes below the knee to alleviate pain in the knee.

Photo 28: Position for pressing fingers into reflexes to stop pain in knee.

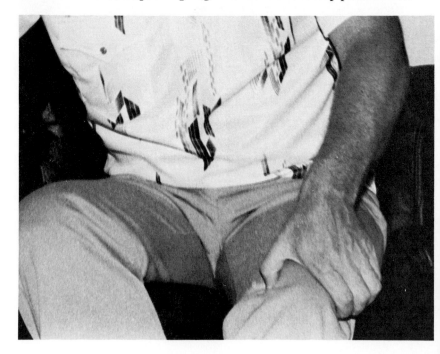

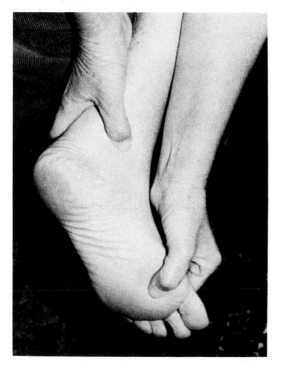

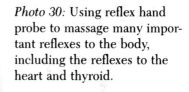

Photo 29: Position for massaging the reflexes in the feet to stimulate the thyroid gland.

Photo 30: Using reflex hand probe to massage many important reflexes to the body, including the reflexes to the heart and thyroid.

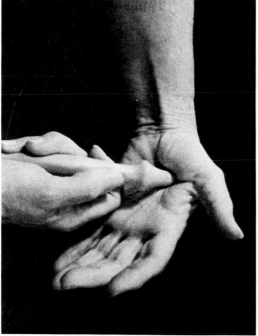

Photo 31: Using the reflex roller massager to stimulate the thyroid gland.

Photo 32: Position for massaging reflexes in the neck and throat to stimulate thyroid and other hormone-producing glands.

Photo 33: Shows an easy method of using the reflex roller to massage the reflexes in the hand.

Photo 34: Organ teacher instructs students on how to use the magic reflex massager before playing a musical instrument. It relaxes the fingers and stimulates the mind.

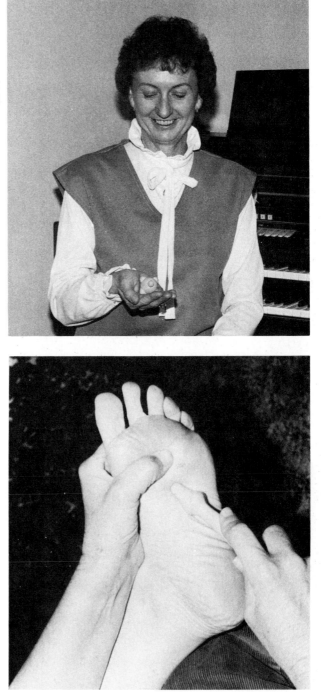

Photo 35: Shows use of the reflex probe to massage reflexes to the adrenal gland and stomach area.

Photo 36: Massaging re-
flexes in the hand to stimulate many parts of the body.

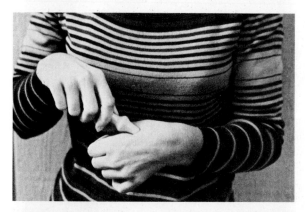

Photo 37: Using reflex hand
probe to stimulate many
parts of the body.

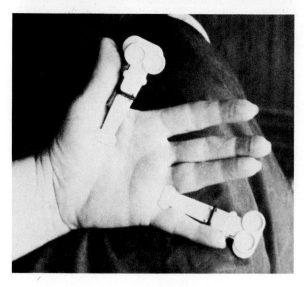

Photo 38: Shows reflex
clamps used on the webs of
the hands, which benefits
many parts of the body.

Photo 39: Position for massaging the reflexes to the gonads, which gives warmth to the system, sparkling eyes, and luminosity.

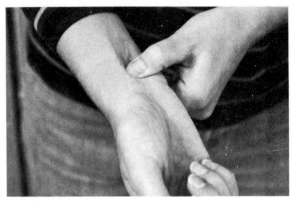

Photo 40: Position for massaging reflexes to reproductive organs and other parts of the body.

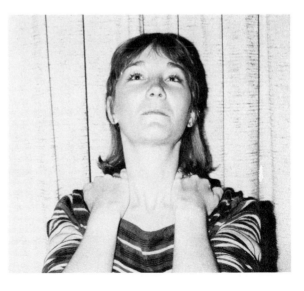

Photo 41: Position for massaging reflexes in the neck and shoulders.

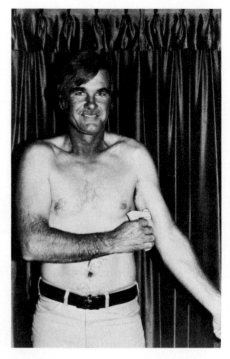

Photo 42: Pinching the little finger on the left hand to help a malfunctioning heart.

Photo 43: Position for massaging the many reflexes in the arm with the reflex roller massager.

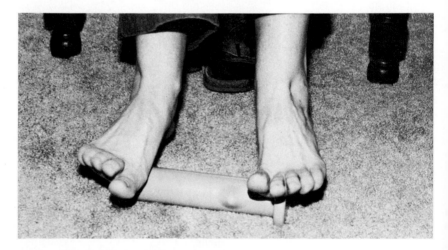

Photo 44: Position for using the reflex foot massager to energize the healing life force into most parts of the body.

Photo 45: Shows comfortable position while using the reflex foot massager to help nature rejuvenate the body naturally.

Photo 46: Shows how to use the reflex roller massager on the feet to help the back and the uterus.

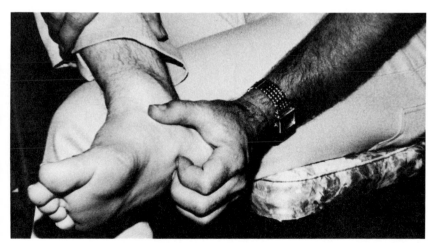

Photo 47: Position for massaging the reflexes under the heel pad to relieve painful problems in the lower half of the body.

Photo 48: Position for massaging reflexes in the hands to overcome back problems.

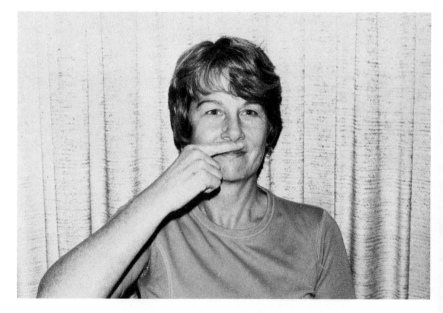

Photo 49: Position for massaging reflexes to spleen and endocrine glands to stimulate beauty and health.

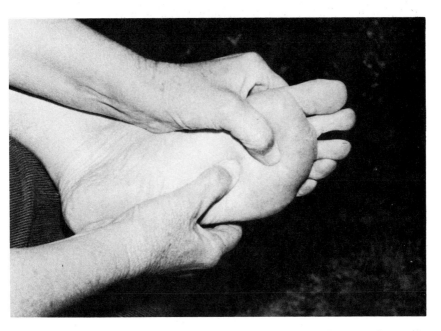

Photo 50: Shows how to use the fingers to massage the reflexes to the kidney and thymus glands in the feet.

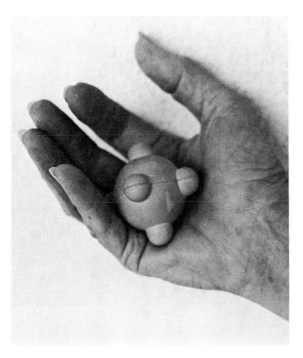

Photo 51: The magic reflex massager, which stimulates most of the glands and organs in the body.

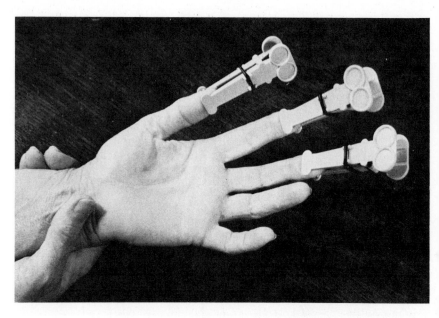

Photo 52: Shows reflex clamps on the first, second, and third fingers of the left hand to anesthetize zones 1, 2, and 3 of the body. See Diagram 16.

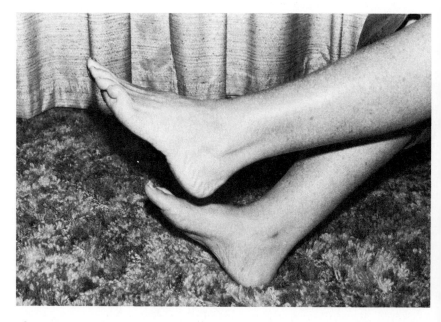

Photo 53: Pounding heels on the floor to stimulate circulation of energy throughout the body.

Photo 54: Position for massage of the reflexes in the head by another person.

Photo 55: Position for massaging reflex to overcome impotency.

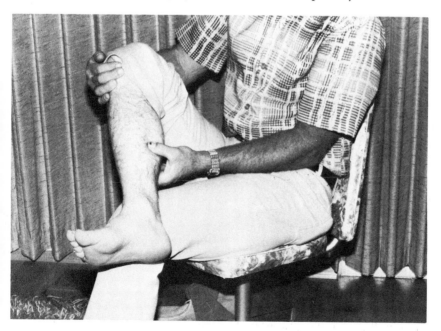

Photo 56: Position for massaging reflexes to the bronchial tubes.

Photo 57: Kneeling position to cure a sore throat.

Photo 58: Organist massages reflexes in the thumb to relax nerves and stop a headache.

Photo 59: Position for pulling the thumb back to help stop a seizure.

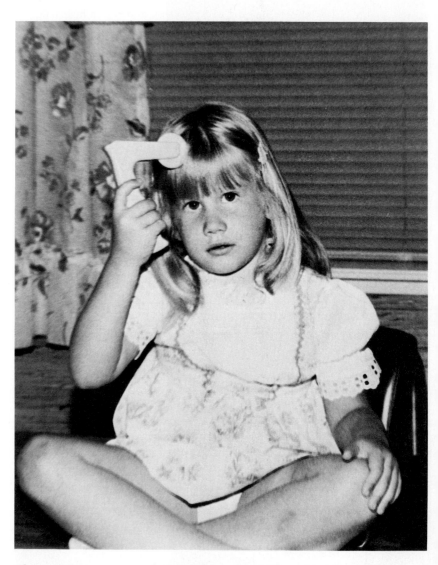

Photo 60: Let us start early in teaching our children the natural way to health through the use of reflexology.

Photo 61: Using the reflex hand probe to massage the reflexes in the thumb to stimulate the pineal and pituitary glands.

Photo 62: Baby enjoys sterilized magic reflex massager as a toy and as a help in cutting a new tooth.

Photo 63: Shows reflex clamp on the third, fourth, and fifth fingers to stimu-late or anesthetize the outer part of the head and body.

Photo 64: The numbers on the face indicate how you can give yourself a reflexology "face lift" at home by pressing and tapping certain reflex buttons.

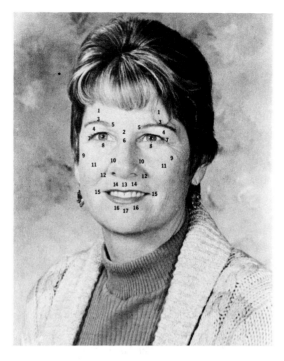

Photo 65: The numbers on the face indicate special reflex buttons that will aid in developing a beautiful complexion.

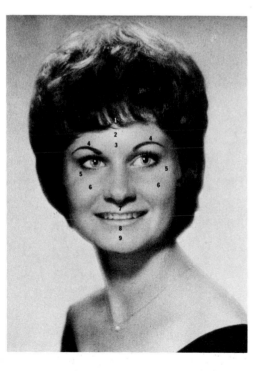

Photo 66: One position for massaging the breast to help develop more beautiful busts.

8

Diet, Vitamins, and Reflexology

When I was first introduced to the wonderful healing method of reflexology, I was told not to recommend any other type of healing as this would confuse people and they would not give credit to reflex massage when they recovered from illnesses. Before studying reflexology, I had been studying nutrition for several years because of my husband's early heart attack, so I did recommend what I had learned of diet and nutrition. I did not follow my teacher's instruction in this matter, and I have never recommended reflexology as the *only* healing therapy.

Dr. Gaylord Hauser, famous nutritionist, tells us that as a young boy he lay dying in a hospital in Chicago; he had undergone many operations and injections for a tubercular hip which refused to heal. Finally, the doctors told his parents to take him home as there was nothing more they could do for him. So he was sent home to die in the serenity of the Swiss mountains. There an old man came to visit and told him that only living foods can make a living body. This man knew nothing about vitamins, proteins, minerals, and other nutrients, but the boy listened and followed the old man's advice by eating enormous amounts of fresh living foods (raw vegetables and fruit). They saved his life, and I believe that Dr. Hauser, in his nineties, is still enjoying good health in his Swiss mountains.

BREWER'S YEAST: WONDER FOOD

Dr. Hauser recommends brewer's yeast, which contains seventeen different vitamins, including all of the B family; sixteen amino acids; and fourteen minerals, including the "trace" minerals held to be essential. It also contains 36 percent protein (sirloin steak may contain as little as 23 percent protein). Steak contains 22 percent fat, but brewer's yeast only contains 1 percent fat. We are talking about one tablespoon—eight grams—only twenty-two calories.

There are several different varieties now on the market that you may buy at your health food store. Do not confuse this for the yeast that is used in baking. You should never eat fresh yeast that is made for baking!

THE VALUE OF BLACKSTRAP MOLASSES

My next favorite wonder food, recommended by Dr. Hauser, is unsulphured molasses or blackstrap molasses. It has some wonderful healing properties, not only when taken as a food but also when applied to cuts and abrasions.

Blackstrap molasses is very rich in iron and the B vitamins. Do *not* use the kind that is sold any place but at the health food stores. The kind sold elsewhere is made of mostly sugar, which you certainly do not want to use, unless you want to slowly poison your body and destroy your teeth.

Many people cannot tolerate the taste of blackstrap molasses, and I was one of those people. I tried every way to make it palatable because I knew of its high food value. I finally acquired a taste for it by using a very small amount at a time in warm or cold milk or water. It is especially good for children and older people when taken at bedtime in place of a chocolate milk drink, using molasses instead of chocolate. This is a good time to get some added calcium by enriching your drink with powdered milk. We all need as much calcium as we can get.

I have also used blackstrap molasses as an enema for trouble in the colon and as a douche when there was any indication of trouble in that area. It has uncanny healing properties when it is used either internally or externally. It may also be held in the mouth to help alleviate a toothache or sores in the mouth.

Many times when I am overworked and feel washed out, a glass of blackstrap molasses and milk gives me a quick pickup when I don't have time for my reflexology pickup massage. To keep healthy the body needs every type of help that we can give it in these days of poisoned air, polluted and poisoned water, and additives that are put into our foods as natural nutrients are removed.

WHEAT GERM, A WONDER FOOD

Wheat germ is claimed to be worth its weight in gold. It is an outstanding source of vitamins B-1, B-2, B-6, and niacin. One-half cup provides a generous daily allowance of this important vitamin. It is rich in protein and provides nearly three times as much iron as other sources.

Fresh wheat germ is delicious sprinkled over hot or cold cereals. It also adds to the flavor and nutrition of any baked product such as biscuits, bread, cakes, etc., and adds a nutty flavor to fresh fruits and salads.

Wheat germ is a good source of vitamin E, which helps in healing many types of heart problems. So don't neglect to find ways to include wheat germ when preparing meals for your family. Along with reflex massage, this is another health bonus to help you stay young and live a long healthy life. Use raw wheat germ when it is available, and keep it stored in the refrigerator to retain its freshness.

THE WONDER OF YOGURT

Yogurt is credited for the longevity of the Bulgarians and natives of some other countries who retain vigor, vitality, and youth to an extremely advanced age.

It is easily assimilated, contains a high-quality protein, and supplies significant amounts of calcium and riboflavin (vitamin B-2) to the diet. It is an acceptable between-meal snack for a quick pickup and an excellent food to eat before going to bed. One cup of yogurt fortified with powdered skim milk gives you about 7 percent of the calories, 17 percent of the protein, 50 percent of the calcium, and 30 percent of the vitamin B-2 needed for a day's diet.

According to information from clinical tests, children who are fed yogurt grow much larger than children who did not receive yogurt in their diet. If you want your children to grow into large adults, yogurt may be the answer. If your children are growing too fast, maybe you should not include yogurt in their diets and should give extra attention to the pituitary gland. See Chapter 10 on endocrine glands.

THE IMPORTANCE OF LIQUID GOLDEN OILS
FOR SUSTAINED ENERGY AND SMALLER WAISTLINES

Fat seems to have a bad name these days, but we all need some fat. Do you know that fat is used as a source of sustained energy, as a heat insulation under the skin, and as a padding for the framework to round out the contours of the body?

Dr. Gaylord Hauser tells us that meals containing some fats have greater "staying power" because fat is more slowly digested and absorbed than all other foodstuffs. This is an important point for those wishing to reduce. The stomach feels full and contented for a longer period of time.

Liquid vegetable fats or oils should be used *instead of hard fats*. They should always be purchased at the health food store to assure freshness and should always be kept refrigerated after opening. Not less than one tablespoon a day should be taken, even when reducing. Take vitamin E when using the golden oils.

POWDERED MILK, ALSO A WONDER FOOD

Powdered skim milk is free from animal fat and has many properties that classify it as another wonder food. It supplies you with a high biologic quality of protein, it is rich in calcium and riboflavin (vitamin B-2), and its vital nutritive factors are easily digested. Being a dry powder, it can be kept on hand at all times. It should be kept in a tightly sealed container in the dark to prevent it from becoming lumpy and also to keep it from losing its riboflavin content.

You can mix it for drinking, use it to fortify regular milk, or add it to your baking for calcium benefits to the whole family as recommended by Dr. Hauser.

When recommending milk, I must inform you that the milk that you get out of the store refrigerators can be mucus forming in some people. Like most of our foods, it has been so changed from its natural state by additives and homogenizing that many doctors are advising people not to use it.

Mrs. J. told me that she had a colonic and the doctor was very upset when he found her so full of mucus. He told her, "No more milk products!" She changed to raw vegetable and fruit juices and says she feels like a new person.

My husband could not drink even half a glass of milk without getting a terrible sinus headache. I found some raw, untreated milk in a health food store and had him drink a glass. He never had one bad reaction from the raw milk. We cannot improve on nature.

THE WONDER FOOD CALLED LECITHIN

We could not exist without lecithin (linoleic acid). This nutrient combines with proteins and cholesterol to form structures so basic that there is no life without them. One structure forms the membranes that enclose every living cell. If such a membrane is absent, weak, or faulty in structure, the contents of the cells leak out and the cells die. If the cells die, then the body dies.

Lecithin also forms myelin, a fatty protein substance that sheathes the major nerves of the body, including the spinal cord. If there is damage to this sheath, it can impair the mentality and be a cause of neurological symptoms, even the dread multiple sclerosis. It may be possible that atherosclerosis is also caused by a deficiency of lecithin.

It is said to regulate the coagulation of the blood so that it is neither too fast nor too slow. It guards against coronary thrombosis and strokes by preventing clotting, and it is also effective against ulcers, asthma and other allergic conditions, dental cavities, and acne and other skin disorders. (Lecithin is one of the building blocks of the teeth.)

Danger of Lecithin

Dr. Tappel tells us that lecithin can also be dangerous if taken without the antitoxin, vitamin E. It seems that this very necessary vitamin can become rancid within our bodies. Dr. Tappel states that rancid lecithin can cause damage to the "structural and functional components of the cell," so it is absolutely essential to take vitamin E, and bioflavonoid (found in garlic) as well, when you ingest lecithin. This proves that we do need balanced vitamins and minerals.

We are told of tests that were made on people of different ages who were suffering from loss of memory. When they were given thirty grams of lecithin, their memory improved, some as much as 25 percent. I know that this is true—I tried it on myself and it did give me more mind power. Calcium (bone meal) should also be taken to balance any excess phosphorus from the lecithin.

THE IMPORTANCE OF VITAMIN A

Vitamin A is one of the easiest vitamins to obtain in the diet. It is not lost in cooking or storing and is generally present in the average American diet. Yet, nutritionists find that most people seem to be on the borderline of deficiency.

There are many symptoms of vitamin A deficiency, including night blindness and certain skin diseases.

All symptoms of vitamin A deficiency are quickly relieved by a sufficient amount being added to the diet, but several conditions keep the body from absorbing this vitamin, in which case you will need to ingest more of it. One way to make sure that you get enough vitamin A and vitamin D in your diet is to take cod liver oil daily. They say that halibut liver oil contains about a hundred times as much vitamin A as does cod liver oil.

I gave my children one teaspoon of cod liver oil the first thing in the morning every day from the time they were very young until they left home. I did not know it at that time, but I was doing the right thing by giving it to them on an empty stomach.

Vitamin A and Dry Skin

Dale Alexander tells us that dry skin is a warning sign that something is wrong within the body and it is crying for help. He tells us, "Your skin is the barometer of your health. It mirrors the condition of your whole body."

If you have dry skin, then you have much more than dry skin. You have dryness throughout your body. It is not merely a skin problem; it means that all parts of your body need lubrication. When you have a health problem, the first place it shows is in your skin.

This is why so many people who use reflex massage claim that all symptoms of dry skin disappear after massaging and pressing the buttons to all tender reflexes. They are using the method of reflexology to stimulate the organs and glands within the body that have been sending signals for help by causing dry skin. It means that your whole system is drying out. It means that you are beginning to age before your time. I will tell you more about dry skin and its importance to your health in the chapter on beauty and your skin.

For now, remember the importance of cod liver oil, which lubricates the whole inner body. Mr. Alexander tells us the best way to take it is in a small amount of milk or orange juice one hour before you eat any food or four hours or more after you have eaten. Cod liver oil also gives you vitamin D.

To take cod liver oil, place one teaspoon of the oil in a small bottle, add about two ounces of milk, shake until foamy, and drink (on an empty stomach). Wait one hour before eating. This gives the intestines time to absorb and utilize the cod liver oil before the liver can grab it. If you can't take milk, orange juice may be used instead, but milk is really the best according to Mr. Alexander.

Although cod liver oil has a bad taste, my children never minded it, probably because they had taken it all of their lives. Now you can buy it in several flavors which make it much easier to take. Be sure that it is fresh when you buy it and keep it in the refrigerator after you have opened it.

Insurance Refused Because of Good Health

After my son got married he decided to take out some insurance. After filling out the necessary papers and having an examination, he waited for the final policy but never received it. He discovered that the salesman was questioning a lot of his friends about him and his health. He asked the salesman why he was investigating his private life. The salesman replied: "I thought that you were trying to cover up some kind of an illness because in all my years of selling insurance I have never had anyone who was really as healthy as you claim to be. Never having any ailments beside the normal children's illnesses. Never been to a doctor in your life! It just didn't ring true. I couldn't believe it, so I had to try to prove what you told me." I believe now that the cod liver oil, along with a good natural diet, is the reason my family enjoys perfect health. Of course, since the discovery of reflexology, we all keep healthy and free from illnesses with the added conscientious use of reflex massage.

VITAMIN C, THE MIRACLE VITAMIN

Vitamin C is one of the miracle vitamins in use today. It is inexpensive and available in health food stores, drug stores, and even in grocery stores. Vitamin C is lauded for its wonderful healing power for nearly every illness, including heart disease, strokes, and arthritis.

When vitamin C was first brought to my attention, it was described as preventing and curing colds. I immediately started to use it to stop colds before they actually got started.

Vitamin C Cures Chronic Bronchitis

One day Mrs. G., a friend I was visiting, told me of her family's cold problems. Every winter they spent several weeks in the hospital with flu and congested lungs. Gene, about nine years old, had suffered with bronchitis all his life. I told her about vitamin C and its healing properties, especially for colds. She said she would try it. A few months later, I again went to visit Mrs. G. and she told me what happened with the vitamin C that she had bought. She said that she placed the bottle on the table, but no one took any of the tablets. (A good mother and wife will put vitamins on each person's plate when setting the table—if there are no small children who might accidentally take them—to make sure everyone gets his or her daily food supplement to keep in perfect health.)

One day, Mrs. G. noticed that the vitamin bottle on the table was empty, so she asked Gene about this. He said that since she had told him, "They are good for you and will make you well," he figured he would take them all and get well all at once—and he did get well all at once! The following winter was one of the worst for colds and flu. Mrs. G. told me that they had all spent weeks in the hospital with colds and bronchial infections—but not Gene. He never had a cold or even a sniffle all winter long. His chronic bronchitis never bothered him once. The next time I saw Gene he was in his twenties, and was a big, healthy, strong man who had never had a recurrence of bronchitis since the time he took the whole bottle of vitamin C. I would not advise anyone to take an overdose of any vitamin, but in clinical studies they are proving that megadoses of vitamins are the answer to many puzzling health problems that modern medication will not cure.

Vitamins A and C reduce the damage smoking causes the body. If you can't quit smoking, take more vitamins A and C.

Paavo Airola, a noted nutritionist, says vitamin C is involved in virtually all the functions of your body. It is the most potent antitoxin. It helps your body to protect itself against every stress and every condition threatening your health.

Dr. M. Higuchi, a Japanese researcher, tells us that his studies show a definite relationship between vitamin C levels in the diet and hormone production of the sex glands. He says that older people, particularly, need larger amounts of vitamin C to assure adequate sex hormone production.

When taking any vitamin or mineral tablets, I powder the tablets for better assimilation. To do this, lay the tablet between two sheets of waxed paper and crush with a hammer until it is powdered. Sprinkle on food or put into milk or a drink. I suggest that you experiment on your own to find out how you like to take it best. Some vitamins are available in powdered form.

GARLIC, A MIRACLE FOOD

I must not leave out the importance of garlic. It is known as a miracle vegetable. It has been used for thousands of years by various races and civilizations. Early Egyptians and Hebrews considered garlic a food endowed with divine properties—and it really is. Garlic is rich in several food chemicals as well as vitamins A, B, C, and D. (Vitamin D is the sunshine vitamin so necessary for existence.) It is also rich in sulfur and iodine. All of these help to stimulate the liver and kidneys, eliminate worms from children and pets, and relieve rheumatic and arthritic conditions and many other ailments.

Garlic also contains bioflavonoid, which is needed when you are taking the wonder food lecithin. (There is now a combined garlic and lecithin capsule available.)

I have proved the marvelous healing properties of garlic in my personal life. As a child, I was always ill. No one knew what my problem was. People did not run to doctors then as they do now. They just trusted to a divine protector and nature to heal, and they usually did. Some people did die, but they died naturally, in one piece, at home, in peace.

When we moved to California, I played with some children who were eating bread and butter and garlic. I had never heard of garlic before. When they gave me a bite of their garlic bread, I loved it! I couldn't get enough of it! I ate it constantly, my family putting up with my bad odor. I don't know how long I was on a garlic binge, but I never had a sick spell again. I had a cast-iron stomach and still do.

My mother had high blood pressure until a nature doctor told her to eat lots of garlic, which she did. She took the little bulbs like pills quite often for a few years. She never suffered with high blood pressure again, and she lived into her nineties.

When I went to Alaska, I went to a wonderful woman doctor for a physical examination. When I went back for the results of the tests she had taken, she took my blood pressure and was surprised to see that it was a little high. She said that she didn't believe it was anything to be concerned about. I told her that, usually, when I thought I had high blood pressure, I ate garlic. She whirled around on her stool and looked at me a moment. I thought, "Boy, I sure said the wrong thing this time." But the doctor pointed her finger at me and said, "You just keep taking that garlic." She knew the value of natural remedies and wasn't afraid to say so. I could write an entire book on the value of garlic to your health.

Garlic is also excellent for pets.

Along with garlic, onions are also an excellent blood purifier and are helpful to your health in other ways. Include plenty of garlic and onions in your diet every day, preferably raw.

THE VALUE OF HERBS

I am not going to go into herbs in this book. There are many very wonderful books already on the market by noted herbalists. I do feel that you should understand a little about their importance to your health and well-being. "For every illness there is an herb." I know that this is true. I have used herbs for years. Herbs cured my late husband of his heart trouble. They were introduced to us by Dewy Conway, an Indian herb doctor in Chico, California.

When you make herb tea, *do not boil it*. Honey and lemon may be added if desired. My favorite herb tea is sage and rosemary. This is good to strengthen many parts of the body. It has a cool fresh taste and leaves the stomach feeling clean and refreshed. A little peppermint may be added if desired. This herb tea is very relaxing, so it is a good drink to take before going to bed. Ask the salesperson at your health food store about herbs and their uses.

DANGERS OF TOO MUCH PROTEIN

Eating lots of protein used to be recommended. But I have always contended that we eat too much protein.

We are all familiar with the health and longevity of the Hunzas. In the last few years, several of our leading biologically and nutritionally oriented doctors have traveled to the valley of the Hunzas and studied the people and their diets. Their diet consists mostly of vegetables and fruit, with very low protein consumption, and they enjoy health and vitality past their one-hundredth birthdays. We stand in envy and awe and wonder what happened to *us*.

The Max Planck Institute in Germany and the Russian Institute for Nutritional Research tell us that too much protein in the diet is extremely dangerous and can cause health disturbances and serious diseases.

We hear about women dying from going on a high-protein weight-reducing diet. I can tell you of a personal experience with a liquid high-protein diet. You should know that I will not recommend anything that I do not try myself first. This powdered protein sounded good—it was made up of all natural grains, nuts, etc., but before I would recommend it, I had to try it myself. I did—and it nearly killed me! In three days, I started to feel bad; then, I developed terrible pains in my back muscles; before I realized what was happening, the tightness in my back muscles continued on around my body to my lungs, so I could hardly breathe. The pain was continuous, but I was able to control it, somewhat, with the reflex clamps and the reflex comb, massaging the endocrine glands reflexes. If I had not gone to an excellent chiropractor, who is also a naturopathic doctor, I am sure I would have died. I can certainly understand why so many people die who go on these high-protein diets and then, in desperation, turn to their medical doctors who may not understand nutrition and are helpless, not knowing what to do. I was put on a lemon juice diet.

The common belief that only animal proteins are complete and that all vegetable proteins are incomplete is false. Too much protein can cause a severe deficiency of magnesium and vitamins B-6 and B-3; also, too much animal protein may be the cause of such diseases as arthritis, osteoporosis, and heart disease. It can also cause mental disorders, particularly schizophrenia. Too much animal protein leads to premature aging caused by a chemical imbalance, overacidity in tissues, intestinal putrefaction, constipation, and degeneration of vital organs.

Dr. Nathan Pritikin tells us why a high-protein diet is harmful: When your protein intake exceeeds approximately 16 percent of your caloric intake of about 3,200 calories, you go into a negative mineral balance. He tells us that almost everyone on the average American diet is in a negative mineral balance. This means that your body is actually losing its precious stores of important minerals such as calcium, iron, zinc, phosphorus, and magnesium. Even though some people take mineral supplements, it does not always remedy this loss of life-sustaining minerals.

Too much protein along with sugar and honey can raise insulin levels dangerously, and it can raise uric acid levels, creating a risk of gout.

When tested on animals, it was learned that when the protein was reduced the animals developed a greater resistance to certain blood and breast cancers. When protein in rodent feed was cut from 26 percent to 4 percent, both rats and mice lived longer and healthier lives.

ELECTRICAL VIBRATIONS FROM LIVE FOOD AFFECT YOUR HEALTH

Any cooked food is dead food. How can you have healthy live cells if you feed them dead foods? The sure and proven way to keep healthy and stay young longer is to eat mostly live foods—raw or lightly steamed vegetables, fresh fruits, seeds, nuts, grains, and especially sprouted seeds like alfalfa or bean sprouts.

Live food has a vibratory rate that generates life! Take, for instance, calcium found in chalk—it has little life vibration that we can use. Then, take the calcium found in cabbage or turnip greens. This calcium has a vibrant life, biochemical activity. This calcium is life-giving. This holds true in all of the live foods that grow. When they are overcooked or sit on the shelves of the market, they lose some of the electrical vibratory life energy.

This electrical vibratory life is created through the activity of sun, air, and water. It takes a living thing to keep another living thing alive.

9

How to Conquer Arthritis with Reflexology

Arthritis is one of the most disabling and painful illnesses and is suffered by people of all ages, even in our age of miracle advances. Scientists can go to the moon, and they can take pictures of distant planets, but they tell us they still have no cure for the painful, crippling ravages of arthritis.

So let us turn back to the simplicity of nature for help. Let us use the magic of reflexology. I have had such wonderful success in relieving people who are seemingly cursed with this disease that I wish I could tell this wonderful news to every arthritic sufferer in the world. I am making some progress in spreading this news, as I receive many letters almost every day from grateful people from most every country in the world who have used my other reflexology books. They thank me for my guidance in bringing them unbelievable relief.

How Mr. A. Helped Himself

Mr. A phoned me from a distant state and said, "May God bless you forever for the new hope that your wonderful book has given to me and my family. Arthritis seems to run in our family, and doctors have told us there was nothing they could do except give us drugs, which bring little or no relief. I could stand the suffering for myself, but to watch it attack my little children one by one has been the hardest for me to bear.

"One day a friend loaned me your book *Helping Yourself with Foot Reflexology.* I started to massage my feet and almost immediately felt the difference in my body. It was like I had suddenly gotten a recharge for a worn-out battery.

"I immediately went to work on my children's feet. Even though it was very painful to them, they seemed to realize that some miracle of nature was at work. (Children have a natural instinct about things like this until we adults destroy their relation with nature.) I am recovering very rapidly. Every day I am better and have a feeling of magnetic vigor which I haven't felt for years. My children are almost back to normal and can once again play with other normal children."

CHILDREN CAN GIVE TREATMENTS

I find that children seemed to turn instinctively to reflexology once it has been introduced to them. I have known of children who loved to work on the feet of their parents and each other, finding the tender reflexes and relating which gland in the body corresponds to each reflex. My books on reflexology are used in many youth camps, and reflexology is taught and practiced by many Boy Scout, Campfire Girl, 4-H, and other youth groups.

VITAMIN C, BACTERIA, AND ARTHRITIS

Lack of vitamins also plays a large part in the development of arthritis. Experimenters have found that, by depriving animals of vitamin C over a period of weeks and then introducing bacteria into them, arthritis was produced. The bacteria were carried by the bloodstream throughout the body and lodged in the small joints first. Then the body tried desperately to stop the infection by depositing calcium all around it. Arthritic stiffness, pain, and swelling resulted. When bacteria were injected into animals that were on balanced diets with plenty of vitamin C, the bacteria did not enter the bloodstream but formed an abscess at the point of infection. The abscess and the bacteria drained off.

NEVER ACCEPT DEFEAT

I do not want you to accept defeat in regard to any *seemingly* hopeless ailment. Not even to so serious a problem as arthritis. There is always hope!

At this point, learn what to do to relieve the ravages of painful arthritis, maybe for yourself, or a loved one, or a friend. Let us turn to the magic of pressing special reflex buttons to awaken healing electrical life force to all areas of the degenerated joint tissues which have been caused by nutritional deficiencies and other causes throughout the years.

HOW TO USE DEEP MUSCLE THERAPY FOR ARTHRITIS

In Canada a woman has been curing arthritis patients for years with what she calls muscle therapy. Therese Pfrimmer discovered this technique by curing herself after becoming paralyzed from the waist down. She tells us that there is no such thing as a *dead* muscle or nerve. The muscles become tight from overwork. They become tense, the blood supply shuts off, and the muscles become sealed off from the rest of the circulation.

This theory is not unlike reflex massage except that you dig in deeper, reaching through to the very muscles that lie against the bone in many cases. Sometimes these muscles will feel like hard rocks that cannot be brought back to life. But all they need is to receive the circulation of blood back into them, and they will return to normal and you will be free from the ravages of painful and crippling disease.

MUSCLES, NOT NERVES, CAUSE CRIPPLING

Muscles should be soft and supple, but in tests of the muscle tone of paralyzed people certain muscles are found to be tough, dry, and hardened; the muscle fibers are stuck together and can't be separated. Therese Pfrimmer says that the crippling problems are in the muscles and not the nerves. Paralysis sets in because the muscles become sealed off from the bloodstream. When fresh oxygenated arterial blood is sealed off, the muscles start to degenerate and become hardened. The muscles are also cut off from the flow of lymph—a fluid that lubricates the muscles and keeps them from sticking to each other. Without lymph there is friction and different muscles that should be free and able to move separately stick together.

Deep muscle therapy can be used for seemingly incurable illnesses. It can be used along with reflex massage to bring faster and even more rewarding results, especially in cases where the muscles have become degenerated. I believe that no muscle or nerve is ever dead; it is just strangled by lack of circulation and *can* be brought back to life and health by releasing the flow of lymph and blood back into it. But exercise and physical therapy alone cannot cure a crippling condition where muscles have become hardened. They must be massaged, and the massage must be done in a certain way.

Suppose some of the muscles have been deprived of a supply of vital electrical energy for a long time. The blood supply has slowly been lessened to certain areas of the body. The muscles have become less and less pliable and more painful. When the muscles cannot move a joint, pain and inflammation occur because the muscles are pulling on the joint tissues. When you release the muscles, the joint will repair itself, and pain and stiffness will disappear. In cases such as this, it is often too late for reflexology alone to benefit, so we will turn to the sensational healing principle of deep muscle massage.

HOW DEEP MUSCLE MASSAGE HELPS ARTHRITIS

Here we will deviate a little from the way I have instructed you to use reflex massage. To help get the circulation back into degenerated muscles, we are going to have to reach in deep and massage them back to life. I believe that no muscle or nerve is *dead* as long as you are *alive*. But, after years of being denied the life-giving flow of blood and lymph, they may have become hard and fibrous. To get these muscles back into their natural state of pliability, we must massage them back to life. In some cases, it may not be easy and it may take time to get complete relief, but it will be worth your effort. In many cases, you will feel results almost immediately.

Now, to start using the muscle massage you will press with the fingers wherever the arthritis is bothering you. Take the fingers and press into or near the affected area of the arms or the legs or other parts of the body. Are the muscles soft and pliable, or are they hard against the bone? To massage these areas correctly, dig the fingers into the flesh and reach the muscle lying against the bone, if that is where it feels tight and hard. Start kneading across the muscles—not with them but across them, as if you were pulling across the strings of a guitar, only with a deep massaging motion. This may be painful, but it is the only way to get the flow of blood back into muscles that have become badly degenerated.

Therese Pfrimmer tells us that we must work on the second and third layers of muscles, not just the muscles lying under the skin which are usually treated by regular massage. Remember, we are not just pressing buttons here as in the technique of reflex massage.

THE IMPORTANCE OF THE ENDOCRINE SYSTEM

We look to the endocrine glands in treating the underlying cause of arthritis. When any one or more of these glands are not functioning to their full capacity, there is trouble elsewhere in the body. Look again at Diagram 5; then turn to Diagram 2 and notice where the endocrine reflexes are on the head. You will find the reflexes to the pituitary and the pineal glands located in the center of the forehead and under the nose. Gonad (sex gland) reflexes are at the top of the head and the center of the chin. The adrenal and pancreas reflexes are also located near the top of the head. Also see the reflex buttons to the triple warmer reflexes shown in Diagram 4.

Using all of the fingers as shown in Photos 4, 6, 7, and 8, press these reflexes with a steady pressure, holding to a slow count of seven. Now, with the middle finger of each hand, press and massage each reflex button that feels sensitive to the touch. Try to follow the reflexes illustrated on the diagrams as much as possible.

Now, let us look at Diagrams 10 and 11 showing the location of the endocrine reflexes on the body. Press these with the fingers or a hand reflex massager, or stimulate a lot of these by using the helpful reflex roller.

HOW TO STIMULATE NATURAL CORTISONE

Cortisone is a drug used to stop pain of many causes. When we massage the reflexes to certain glands, we stimulate these glands into releasing a form of *natural* cortisone into the bloodstream. We are all aware of the damaging side effects that synthetic cortisone has on the body when it is injected. The natural cortisone produced by our glands alleviates pain quickly without any harmful side effects.

See Diagram 9. Notice a point between the first and second lumbar vertebrae near the lower part of the back. Press this point, using a gentle pressure to start, increasing it gradually for about seven seconds. This will cause a gland to secrete a natural human cortisone.

Most of you will not know exactly where the first and second lumbar vertebrae are located, but if you will start by placing your fingers on the tail bone and then pressing gently on each vertebra, you will feel a very sensitive spot about three finger widths up from the end of the spine. Use a press-and-hold on this, about three times, and your pain will vanish as if by magic. You may use this for any ailment in which cortisone is helpful. This is especially good for arthritis in various parts of the body, and also asthma and bursitis.

This is another proof that your body has the capacity to cure itself of any ailment that might attack it when given a little help from nature.

Bursitis and Arthritis Alleviated

Dear Mrs. Carter,

Reflexology is the most wonderful and natural way of healing I ever dreamed of. I have been taking these treatments for about five years and have been giving them for over two years to friends and neighbors. What really made a believer out of me was this: I had bursitis in my shoulder; also, I have had two pins in one ankle for over twenty years. The ankle was very sore. I had lots of pain and swelling. After two treatments my shoulder was fine, and after three treatments my ankle was much better. Now I have no trouble with it at all.

—Mrs. N. P.

Another Arthritis Sufferer Helped

Dear Mrs. Carter,

I want to tell you of the wonderful results I have gotten from reflexology.

I had arthritis ever since I was seventeen years old and now I am forty-six years old; this is the first time that I am without pain. Plus, my husband was losing all his hair and after doing the hand reflexology as you directed, his hair stopped falling and is now growing back. I want to thank you very much and God bless you.

—I. A.

SPECIAL REFLEXES FOR HIP AND SCIATICA

To relieve many types of pain in the legs and the hips, press on the reflexes around the hip socket. For arthritis pain, search for a very tender reflex on the outer edge of the buttocks.

Since everyone's body is different, you will have to search for these tender reflexes. You may find several sore buttons in this area. When you press on an "ouch" reflex, hold pressure on it as you have been directed to when massaging other reflex buttons. Using the reflex roller massager will be helpful here in locating the tender reflex buttons.

For sciatica pain, which can be excruciating, look first to the pad in your heel. You will probably have to use the reflex hand probe or another blunt device for this reflex button. If your problem is from sciatica, you will have no trouble locating the sore spot in the heel pad. It will be very painful, but by holding pressure on it or massaging it, you will be relieved of all sciatica pain.

Now turn to another reflex to relieve sciatica near the hip joint. Move the leg and find where the hip socket moves; press around in this area until you find a very tender button. Press and hold this with the thumb or finger. It will feel as if you are holding a red-hot poker into your hip, but it will relieve the pain of your sciatica.

Massage Brings Comfort

Dear Mrs. Carter,

Since he got bacterial meningitis in 1975, my husband has gone steadily downhill. We were at a dead end with doctors. Two weeks ago I started to use reflexology. Four days ago he started to be able to reach the back of his neck with both arms. He had not been able to do this for over two years. His color is better and his depression has much improved. His whole system seems now to be on the mend. Until reflexology I really feared for his sanity. Thanks to God, good food, vitamins, common sense, and reflexology, we are now in better health than we have been in years. God bless you.

—C. U. D.

Dear Mrs. Carter,

I have had low blood sugar for several years. I have never really known that glowing feeling of good health. Then I found your book on reflexology, and by using the methods described I do feel much better. Lately I have had some bouts with arthritis and then after studying your book I discovered that the two ailments are interrelated. The massage and the clamps have brought immeasurable comfort and ease. I am still looking for a panacea for an abundance of pep and I hope to attain it with the help of the magic massagers.

—G. A. R.

REFLEXOLOGY FOR THE KNEES

I have had many people come to me with painful knees. It seems that for no known reason the knees become painful, and nothing seems to bring relief. But, they have never tried the miracle power of using reflexology to cure their knee problems.

A Dancer's Problem Solved

I was at a dance not long ago where a friend kept wanting me to dance with her husband. She finally told me that she was having trouble with her knees and that they were becoming worse all the time. She was afraid that they might have to give up square dancing, which was their main source of exercise. I laid my hand on her knee and pressed with the thumb and middle finger about two inches above the kneecap (see Diagram 9C and Photos 27 and 28) for a few seconds. She was amazed to find the pain gone, and she danced the rest of the evening. I talked to her several days later. When asked about her knees, she admitted she had forgotten she ever had a problem with her knees.

Before I learned of reflexology, I used to use hot vinegar packs to stop knee pain. These can also be used in conjunction with the reflexology treatment, if needed. So far, I have not known anyone to need further treatment for painful knees after a correct reflexology treatment—pressing the reflex buttons above and below the knees.

The Function of Your Knees

Did you ever take time to think how much work the knees do? They are truly an intricate marvel of God's design, as is our whole body. No wonder that sometimes these overused parts seem to wear down, which is especially true with athletes. They should all learn to send a renewed electrical supply to weakening areas. By knowing what buttons to press to open up a larger supply of energy and renew the life force into the malfunctioning knee, a person can enable it to return to normal.

Quick Relief for a Knee Problem

My son-in-law told me how much he had been suffering from pain in his knees when I was visiting last year. Since he works mainly at a desk, his problem was not caused by too much exercise (maybe by not enough exercise). I walked over to where he was sitting rubbing his knees, laid my hand on one knee, and pressed with my thumb and finger just above the kneecap for about seven seconds. Then I pressed on the reflexes just below the kneecap for the same amount of time.

I used this method on both knees, and he couldn't believe that they had stopped hurting. I showed him how to do this on himself if the trouble came back. That was well over a year ago. He has not had to use the reflex massage on himself because his knees have never hurt him since the one treatment.

HOW TO MASSAGE KNEE REFLEXES

To give yourself a treatment for painful knees, take the thumb and middle finger of the right hand and, just above the knee bone on each side of the right knee where the bone ends, feel a soft spot. It will probably be quite tender when pressed. Now press and hold this with as much pressure as you can stand for about seven seconds.

Now go to the reflex buttons below the knee. You will do the same pressing and feeling as you did above the knee. Find the soft spot or indentation just below the knee bone with the thumb and middle finger. This will probably be quite tender. Press and hold for about seven seconds. Follow the same procedure on the left knee. This is usually all you need to do to end pain in the knees.

10

How Reflexology Stimulates the Endocrine Glands

The endocrine glands have no ducts and secrete their hormones directly into the bloodstream. If you will look at Diagram 5, you will see the most important endocrine glands as they are located in the body. To those who study the esoteric teachings, these are referred to as *chakras*.

The pituitary gland is located near the center of the head, along with the pineal gland. The thyroid and parathyroids are near the larynx at the base of the neck. The thymus is located in the chest area. The pancreas is lower in the body under the stomach and above the adrenals (or superadrenals) which are like little caps on the kidneys. Then, we move down to the lower area of the body to the gonads or sex glands (testes and ovaries) of men and women.

THE IMPORTANCE OF THE ENDOCRINE GLANDS

All of these glands supplement and interact with each other. Their normal development and functions are of great importance to the well-being of every individual. The hormones that they secrete are responsible for the difference between a dwarf or a giant, a genius or an imbecile, a happy or a cheerless individual. They control what we are—our energy, activity, radiance, and stabilization as well as the vitalization of the life processes. Their influence is pervasive in all that we do and are. They are responsible for determining the forms of our bodies and the working of our minds.

THE PITUITARY

A person who is relaxed and generally happy, without any frustrations, is sure to possess a normal, healthy pituitary gland. If you are not all of these, then you should check the reflexes to the pituitary gland, located in the center of the pad of the big toe and the center of the pad on the thumb. See Diagram 5. You will also find reflex buttons to the pituitary located on the forehead. See Diagram 2. This gland also helps prevent an excessive accumulation of fat. If you are trying to lose weight, there is reason for you to give the reflexes to the pituitary gland special attention.

Several years ago, an experiment was made by Rowe, in which he found that disobedience, bullying, moroseness, and many types of child delinquency were caused by a faulty pituitary gland.

The pituitary gland is likened to a first violin in keeping the body in harmony. If it is out of tune, the whole body is out of harmony, and no one can feel in top condition if his or her glands are not *all* in tune with each other. This gland is responsible for the proper growth of our body glands and organs, including normal sexual development.

The pituitary gland is one of the controllers of growth, so if you are concerned about the growth rate of your child, be sure to massage the reflexes to your child's pituitary gland. This will stabilize the growth rate to normal whether your child is growing too fast or too slow. If this area is tender, it should be massaged often. Teach children to massage this special button for themselves and hopefully they will teach their classmates the miracle of massaging their own reflexes to help keep their growth rate normal and learn to use it in helping other malfunctioning areas as well.

THE PINEAL GLAND

The pineal gland controls the development of the other glands, keeping them in their proper range. The malfunction of this gland influences the sex glands, causing the premature development of the entire system. This gland keeps the normal activity of the endocrine system harmonious and effective.

THE THYROID GLAND

The degree of thyroid activity makes a person either dull or alert, animated or depressed, quick or slow. The development and activity of the sex glands also depends on a normal and healthy thyroid.

The important reflexes for the thyroid gland are located in the hands and the feet. Find the reflex to the thyroid gland just under the large pads near the big toes. These will be on both feet. The reflexes on the left foot stimulate the thyroid on the left side and those on the right foot stimulate the thyroid on the right side. This is also true of the reflexes on the hands near the thumbs. See Diagram 5.

Use the thumb, the fingers, or a reflex massager and press in under the foot pads and hand pads. See Photos 29 and 30. You will probably find some very tender buttons in this area, so you must massage the soreness out—but not all at once. Send these healing life forces to the malfunctioning thyroid a little at a time until it once again returns to a normal and healthy working order.

Now, we will look to the reflexes for the thyroids in other parts of the body. As you look at Diagrams 5 and 13, you can see that the thyroids are located on each side of the throat, and in Diagrams 10 and 11 you will see that the reflexes to the thyroids are located on the neck. See Photo 31 to learn the positions for massaging the reflexes to these important glands. Place the fingers on one side of the throat and the thumb on the opposite side. See Photo 32. Now, starting close to the jaw, use a gentle rolling motion with the fingers. You need not press hard here—we do not want to bruise the thyroids in any way. Use this rolling massage, working down to the collar bone. Now use this same rolling massage and work back up to the jaw bone. Now change hands so that the thumb will be on the opposite side of the throat and again go through the same procedure, massaging down to the collar bone and back up to the jaw. I would advise you to go slowly and do this once or twice the first day. Increase the amount of time you spend doing this massage gradually as you feel it is necessary.

Look at Photo 25 to see how the thumbs are hooked under the jaw bone and chin. This should be done with a gentle pressing motion two or three times on each side. These particular reflexes will, when stimulated by massage as I showed you, develop beautifully firm and smooth skin, of which I will tell you more in the chapter on beauty. It is also said to keep the hair from turning gray.

Let us look at one more reflex to the thyroid gland. If you try to find the very center of the top of your head, you find a sensitive reflex to the thyroid glands. See Photo 8. This, of course, will stimulate parathyroids also. It should be located on a straight line from the front of the ears. Feel for it—every head is shaped differently. Now, place the middle fingers of both hands on this reflex and hold it for a few seconds, then release. Do this three times—not any more than that at first. The middle finger of one hand may be used if you feel you could get better results.

THE PARATHYROIDS

The parathyroids, four tiny bead-sized glands embedded in the surface of the thyroid, carry an enormous responsibility in keeping your body functioning in perfect order. The normal functioning of these glands results in poise and tranquility. They influence the stability within your body and the maintenance of its metabolic equilibrium by controlling the distribution and activity of calcium and phosphorus in the system. These represent a certain polarity— phosphorus being connected with the nervous system, calcium with the skeletal. I hope you will recognize the dynamic factor we have on one side and the static one on the other. The parathyroids maintain a balance between them.

The reflexes to these all-important little glands are located in about the same area as the thyroid reflexes on the hands and the feet except you will have to press in more deeply for the parathyroids. From what I have just told you about these glands, you will recognize how important it is to keep them functioning in perfect order at all times. You will probably have to use the little hand massager to reach in deeply enough to stimulate them with renewed electric life force. See Photo 30. As you massage the reflexes on the hands and the feet, you may find them extremely tender. You must give them special attention until they are no longer so painful when pressed with the massager.

Some people always have a certain amount of tenderness to the reflexes in the parathyroid areas, so you will be wise in massaging them each time you give yourself a treatment.

THE THYMUS GLAND

In the second century, Galen gave the name *thymus* to the pinkish-gray, two-lobed organ in the chest. The thymus is located high in the chest behind the breast bone. See Diagrams 10 and 11. The function of the thymus was a mystery to medical doctors until the 1950s. Yet in 1902, Foulerton, a London physician, was using thymus extract in the treatment of cancer.

There has been a misconception concerning the role the thymus plays in our overall health. It was believed that the thymus diminishes in size as we reach puberty and becomes useless, which has been proven to be untrue by Dr. John Diamond. In his book, *Your Body*

Doesn't Lie, he tells us, "The thymus can be considered to be a true endocrine gland—that is, an organ that secretes a hormone into the bloodstream to be carried to another part of the body where it will have its effect."

Dr. Diamond tells us, "The evidence accumulated over the last twenty years on the thymus gland's role in immunology is overwhelming. In a human being or an animal in which the thymus gland has been removed or destroyed, there is a loss of effectiveness of the immune mechanisms of the body that guard against infection and cancerous growths."

People become more susceptible to all types of diseases as they become older because they let the thymus become weak. It may be the most important gland in your body; it is the seat of life energy. When the thymus becomes weak you lose energy.

The thymus gland is involved with the strength of muscular contraction and can be tested by using applied kinesiology (which can also be used to overcome stress or determine the cause of it).

The thymus is involved in the flow of lymph throughout the body. The lymphatic system drains foreign matter, cellular debris, and toxins from the cells and carries them to the bloodstream for disposal.

The Thymus Is the Home Base of Energy

The thymus gland monitors and regulates energy flow throughout the body energy system, initiating instantaneous corrections to overcome imbalances as they occur so as to achieve a rebalancing and harmony of body energy.

Dr. Diamond also tells us, "The thymus gland is the link between mind and body, being the first organ to be affected by mental attitudes and stress!"

We learn that many things in life can so deplete our energy that they cause all of the muscles in our body to go weak; these include the wrong kind of food, sugar, and chemical additives. Sitting on a soft seat, especially in a car, can cause us to be less mentally alert by weakening our minds and our muscles. Just being near certain people can drain our energy. Negative thoughts, loud or inharmonious music, and certain colors can also deplete our energy, as does continual stress.

How to Reactivate the Thymus

Let me tell you how you can use reflexology to reactivate the energy in the thymus gland quickly, thus strengthening the weakened muscles in the body. See Diagrams 5, 10, and 11 and note the location of the thymus gland in the chest. If you take the ends of the fingers and tap the chest several times over the thymus gland, you will stimulate the gland so that it will send quick energy to all of the body muscles.

An inconspicuous way to activate the thymus back to quick normal activity is to press a reflex to the thymus which is located in the roof of your mouth just in front of the teeth. Press this reflex with the tip of your tongue.

How to Test with Kinesiology

Let us test the power of the thymus over the weakening and the strengthening of the muscles by the short and simple method of kinesiology. This testing will take two people. Have someone stand in front of you with his or her left arm held out parallel to the floor while his right arm is relaxed at his side. Either arm may be used. Now, standing in front of the person, place your left hand on his shoulder to steady him. Tell him that you are going to press down the arm he is holding out straight and that he is to resist. Place your right hand on his arm just above the wrist. Press his arm firmly, just enough to test the strength of his muscles. This is not a contest of strength. If the arm is weak, have him tap the thymus reflex on his chest or press the thymus reflex in front of the teeth in the center of the roof of his mouth with the tip of his tongue, and test again. The muscles should now be strong.

While his muscles are strong, have him put a little sugar in his mouth, think of an unpleasant situation, listen to inharmonious music or sounds, or perform another stress-causing action before he tries the test again. If you are doing this correctly, the muscles will have become very weak and he will not be able to resist a slight pressure. Think of all the muscles in your body losing energy and becoming weak so quickly from such a slight cause of stress. Do you wonder why so many people are upset and ill without knowing why?

TESTING FOR POSITIVE LIFE ENERGY

Now let us turn to positive things that will reactivate your thymus into raising your life energy rather than depleting it.

There are many more positive ways to reactivate the thymus than there are negative, so let us learn a few of them. Let us first turn to nature.

Dr. Diamond tells us, "The normal position of the tongue is to keep the tip against the centering reflex in the roof of the mouth at all times. In this position the entire body is tonified through the relationship between the centering reflex button and the body energy system and the life energy." Every time you smile you are also stimulating the reflexes to the thymus gland. Smiling is a body energizer, so think positive thoughts; keep your mind on happy thoughts at all times; feel the vibrations of love for all things beautiful. Sit straight; listen to good music; eat only good natural food. Be thankful and joyful in all things. Do the words "love, faith, hope, and charity" have a deeper meaning for you? Were these words given to us as body energizers as well as for spiritual upliftment?

How to Massage Other Reflexes to the Thymus Gland

Look to another reflex to the thymus that is located in the bottom of the feet. See Diagram 5. You will also find this thymus reflex in the hands. See Photos 33 and 34 for use of the reflex roller and the magic reflex massager to stimulate all reflexes to most of the body located in the hands.

You will also find reflexes to the thymus located in the head. See Diagram 16. Anything on the center line will help stimulate the thymus gland.

I hope you are now more conscious of the importance of the thymus. Square dancers live long healthy lives. They stimulate the thymus with good music, laughter, and fun in their dances. Keep smiling and laughing at all times, thus reactivating your thymus gland into raising your life energy instead of depleting it with negative vibrations.

The Pancreas

The pancreas is a large gland located in the midsection of the body. It is really two glands in one; the major part of the pancreas secretes digestive juices, and certain cells within the pancreas secrete the hormone insulin, which maintains the body's sugar level.

In Diagrams 5, 10, and 12, see the position of the pancreas in relation to other abdominal organs and glands in the body. Notice in Diagram 10 how the reflex to the pancreas is located in about the same position as the reflex to the spleen as shown in Diagram 11. When we massage the reflexes in this area, we will be sending the stimulation of electrical energy into both glands simultaneously.

We will also be stimulating these and other glands as we massage the reflexes to the pancreas located in the hands and the feet. Start on the left foot, and with your thumb or whatever you use to massage the reflexes, start just below the pad of the big toe where we found the thyroid reflexes. See Diagram 5 and Photo 35. With a rolling method, massage clear across the foot, searching for sore buttons. Remember, whenever you find a button that is sensitive to the touch, no matter where it is located (unless it is a bruise or a swollen area), either apply pressure or use the massage technique.

Now turn to the reflex in the hands. Using the thumb or a device with a massaging, pressing motion, massage completely across the center of the opposite hand. Work toward the web between the thumb and the forefinger, searching for tender buttons as you go across the hand. See Diagram 5 and Photos 33 and 35. Do this to both hands two or three times; then, pinch and massage this web in both hands, working clear up between the bones of the thumb and the finger. See Diagrams 9A, D, and E, and Photos 37 and 38. This seems to be a "hot spot" for the reflexes to many parts of the body, so don't neglect it. It aids in causing a full flow of the vital electrical life force, no matter to what part of the body we are attempting to clear the channels.

Turn to Diagram 10; with the fingers of one or both hands, whichever seems to give the best results, press into the area a little below the ribs. Hold to a slow count of three and release. Repeat this three times. Because the pancreas spreads over a large area, you may move the fingers an inch toward the center of the body and repeat almost all the way across.

See Diagram 2 for the location of the reflex buttons on the head and above the lips. There are also reflex buttons in the ears which are not shown, but when you massage the ears you will be stimulating the reflexes to the pancreas.

THE ADRENAL GLANDS

Your glands control every minute of your life from cradle to grave. The adrenal glands promote your inner energy—the drive to action. The adrenal glands consist of two small triangular bodies lying above and in front of the kidneys. The cortex, the outer part of the adrenal, produces three types of hormones that control many functions of the body, including water and salt balances, and carbohydrate, protein, and fat metabolism. The inner part of the adrenal produces the hormone adrenalin, which instantly prepares the body to react to an emergency.

To stimulate the adrenal glands and keep them in perfect working order, first turn to the reflexes located in the hands and the feet. By looking at Diagram 6, you can see that the adrenals are located on top of the kidneys, so the reflexes will be just a little above the kidney reflexes in the center of the hands and a little above the center in the feet. See Diagrams 5 and 6. If this area is tender at all, the adrenals are probably telling you that they are not getting a full supply of energy. Somewhere in the lines the power is getting short-circuited, so you will have to push a few buttons to correct the power shortage. Press and massage these buttons with the thumbs or a reflex massager several times, but be aware that they lie so close to the kidneys that you cannot help but massage the reflexes to the kidneys as well as the adrenal glands. We do not want to overmassage the kidney reflexes in the beginning, so, to start, only massage the adrenals for about five seconds.

Look at Diagram 2 for the location of the adrenal reflexes on the head and Diagrams 10 and 11 for body location. You will see also the kidney reflexes; you have learned that when you massage the reflexes to the kidneys the adrenals are also helped. Press and hold gently on body reflexes shown in Diagrams 10 and 11.

THE GONADS—THE SEX GLANDS

The gonads—in men the testes, in women the ovaries—are located in the lower part of the body. The pituitary gland produces the hormone that activates the gonads to begin puberty. The gonads are responsible for making our personalities radiant and magnetic. They give us the ability to attract people and keep their affection. When the gonads are functioning properly, we will have sparkling eyes, luminosity, self-reliance, and self-assurance. The gonads produce hormones that create the inner warmth in our systems, preventing inflexibility, hardening, and stiffening.

I want you to realize the importance of the endocrine glands and understand how reflexology can normalize their improper functioning. Our glandular system is the transmitter of life forces that are transformed into function throughout the body. By using reflex massage on the reflexes to these glands, we help stimulate the whole body. See Photo 39.

Look at Diagram 5 to find where the gonads are located in the body. In Diagram 7 you will find the reflexes to the gonads located near the ankles on the outside of the feet—the testes for the men and the ovaries for the women. On the inside of the feet (near the ankles) are the reflexes for the uterus in the women and for the penis in the men. This will also be an area to massage for prostate trouble. For the gonad reflexes, you will also pinch and massage the cord up the back of the leg, the Achilles' tendon.

On the hands, find the reflexes that involve the wrists. Search here for tender buttons on all parts of the wrist. When you find a sore button, massage it out. See Diagram 5 and Photo 40.

There are more reflexes that will help the gonads, which I will explain more fully in the chapter on sex and its related problems.

Complete Recovery Through Reflex Massage

While giving a seminar in Alaska on reflexology, I met a very sick lady. By her color I knew she had something seriously wrong. She told me that she had gotten spray poisoning while at work and doctors did not know what to do for her. She suffered most of the time without knowing how to get help. I told her I might be able to help her, as the poison was probably in the lymphatic system. She was willing to try anything to be well again.

I massaged her whole body for two hours at a time, pressing and pulling with my fingertips. I had to extend my stay for a few days, but it was worth it because she recovered almost completely before I left. Now she uses the reflex massage on herself to help free her body of this accumulation of toxic poison.

11

How Reflexology Can Strengthen an Ailing Heart and Blood Circulation

Everyone should be more aware of the heart and how to massage the reflexes to keep it in perfect working condition. All life processes are rhythmic alterations of tension and release of tension. Blood moves from the lungs where it is oxygenated, to the small intestines where it begins to give up oxygen, making these two opposite organs, lungs and the small intestines, the poles. The heart beats as the flow of oxygenated and deoxygenated blood moves through it, creating tension and release of tension. Ancient traditional medicine declares, "The meridian of the heart rules the arteries between the lungs and the small intestines and the lung rules over the heart."

The heart controls the mind. If the heart is weak, like a ruler without power, it invites revolt. When a multitude of body areas are malfunctioning and the problem cannot be pinpointed, it means that the electric life force is not flowing freely through the meridian channels. See Diagram 16.

As we see the roots of the heart in the tongue, a fluent speech may mean a good heart. If a person speaks too much and without pause or if he or she stutters, this could indicate a weak heart. Check this symptom out with reflexology.

A Massage to Help the Heart

Dear Mrs. Carter,

I am seventy-seven years young, and this morning I sure thought my heart was giving up. I massaged the reflexes for a half-hour and, thank God, I am feeling better.

Kindly inform me if I can find a doctor who practices reflexology in my vicinity. Thank you and God bless you and yours.

—Mrs. K. P.

REFLEX POINTS TO HELP THE HEART AND CIRCULATION

No matter what your heart problems might be, reflexology can help. Remember that a malfunctioning heart is usually caused by a problem in some other area of the body.

We are all aware that the heart is the pumping station that keeps the body functioning. Like the pump of a well, if the heart slows down, the circulation of the life lines slows down. The fluid, be it water or blood, will not do a complete job of circulating to all areas needed; thus certain areas which are denied full circulation become weak, and deterioration sets in.

The heart is a strong muscle made to endure with ease and efficiency. By pressing certain reflex buttons located on the feet and the hands and several places on the body, this great muscle can be kept at top efficiency. If it has a malfunction you can help it to function normally by pressing and massaging the heart reflex buttons.

See the reflex buttons near the spine on Diagram 17B. To help an ailing heart you can use these reflexes, but you will need someone else to help you. Just have the person find the tender spots and press or massage until soreness is relieved. If the spine is out of adjustment, your chiropractor can help put it into place. Be careful to get a reputable chiropractor. Some of my chiropractor friends tell me that some chiropractors are becoming "money mad" like some of the medical doctors and give treatments designed to keep you coming back to them.

DEEP MUSCLE THERAPY FOR THE HEART

Deep muscle therapy, according to Mrs. Pfrimmer, also helps the heart. She claims that deep muscle massage has helped all kinds of heart problems. So along with your diet for the heart and reflex massaging of the heart reflexes, you should help the heart by loosening the muscles, by going deeper than the reflexes and massaging the deep muscles that could be causing lack of circulation to the heart.

First work on the muscles of the left arm as this is a major source of blood to the heart. Start massaging these muscles at the wrist of the left arm. You are not massaging reflex buttons here but deep underlying muscles. Remember, as your muscles become tighter, they start strangling you—squeezing your arteries and closing off your circulation.

Massaging Across Muscles

Press in with the fingers, feeling for hard, tight muscles lying along the bone of the arm. Use the tips of the fingers and also the thumb when necessary. *Important:* Massage *across* these muscles (from side to side), not with them as you do in reflex massage. Massage all the way up the arm, working the fingers on all sides of the arm and pressing in as you massage. If you find muscles that feel like steel bands, spend more time on these, but do not overdo it at first.

After you have massaged all the way up the arm, massage the muscles in the neck. See Photo 41. If you find these to be tight, spend some time massaging them to loosen them up. This also will help prevent a stroke by freeing the circulation of fresh blood to the brain. After you get these muscles loosened up, go to the muscles in the chest, especially on the left side. Massage *across* all the muscles in this area starting from the arm, under the arm and shoulder on down across the chest. Work on any muscles that might feel tight to your fingers. If any of these muscles are too tight to loosen with the fingers, use a vinegar pack to help loosen them and increase the circulation.

If it is hard for you to do this deep massage, another person might do it for you with better results. Just remember that tight muscles can cause a heart attack, so, along with the methods of aiding your heart with reflex massage and diet, be sure that you keep these muscles to the heart loose and pliable.

Now let me give you a few hints on diet for your heart.

HOW DIET HELPS THE HEART AND PREVENTS STROKES

The Importance of Vitamin E

Wilfred E. Shute, M.D., tells us in his book, *Vitamin E for Ailing and Healthy Hearts,* that coronary thrombosis, the major cause of heart attack death, is the greatest single killer in the world today. You may be surprised to know that coronary thrombosis was unknown as a disease entity in 1900 and apparently hardly existed at that time.

Dr. Paul Dudley White writes: "When I graduated from medical school in 1911, I had never heard of coronary thrombosis, which is one of the chief threats to life in the United States and Canada today." How do we explain why a disease entity that did not occur prior to 1910 has become a greater ravager of human life than any plague recorded in history?

Historical Cause of Thrombosis Heart Attacks

It is irrefutable that when new and more efficient milling methods were introduced into the manufacture of wheat flour, permitting for the first time the complete stripping away of the highly perishable wheat germ, the diet of western man lost one of its best sources of vitamin E. Flour milling underwent this great change around the turn of the century, and it became general in 1910. For your heart's sake, take vitamin E every day and press heart reflexes as in Photo 13.

Dr. Shute tells us, "Vitamin E is, in addition to its other properties, a superb antithrombin in the bloodstream." Not only will vitamin E dissolve clots, but circulating in the blood of a healthy individual it will prevent thrombi (clots) from forming.

How Vitamin B-6 Prevents Heart Attacks and Strokes

According to research at Harvard University and Massachusetts Institute of Technology (MIT), vitamin B-6 can prevent heart attacks and strokes. Many doctors now claim that cholesterol is not the cause of heart disease and strokes. Experts believe that the real culprit is an amino acid called homocysteine, and that vitamin B-6 eliminates the harmful substance from the body. Dr. Stephen A. Raymond and Dr. Edward R. Gruberg, MIT scientists, have concluded after two years of research that homocysteine, a by-product of high-protein diets, is the key real cause of hardening of the arteries, which in turn causes heart attacks and strokes.

The Power of an Unusual Vitamin

Dr. Gruberg and Dr. Raymond are both neurophysiologists—researchers specializing in the study of the nervous system. To get sufficient vitamin B-6, they say, people should either take B-6 supplements or eat more fruits, vegetables, whole grains, and nuts. At the same time, they should cut down on meat, eggs, and dairy products. When these high-protein foods are digested, the amino acid homocysteine is produced in the blood. Dr. Raymond tells us that homocysteine can harden and narrow the arteries by somehow stimulating the growth of cells along the delicate inner arterial walls.

Vitamin B-6 prevents the accumulation of homocysteine in the blood, thus dramatically reducing the risk of hardening of the arteries, which is the main cause of heart attack and stroke. Studies have shown that people with heart disease tend to have a vitamin B-6 deficiency and to have homocysteine acid in their blood. These doctors believe the Food and Drug Administration's recommended daily allowance of 2 milligrams of B-6 is far too low. They tell us that they supplement their own diets with 25 to 50 milligrams of B-6 daily. If these doctors who have made scientific studies of the importance of vitamin B-6 use it in their own diets, we had better take a hint from the experts and do likewise.

Heart Attacks and Strokes Prevented with a Vitamin

There is a growing belief among doctors that vitamin C can prevent heart attacks and strokes. The studies—one at the Medical University of South Carolina and two at Louisiana State University Medical Center—revealed that vitamin C reduces the tendency of blood platelets to stick together and cause clots.

Researchers note that this tendency, which is called "platelet aggregation," contributes to heart attacks and strokes. In the South Carolina study, Dr. Kay Sarji and fellow researchers gave eight healthy volunteers two grams of vitamin C daily for seven days. Blood was drawn before and after the test. Clotting agents were mixed with it and the clotting of the blood was measured. In most cases the platelet aggregation was reduced by more than 50 percent.

Miracles by Another Vitamin

Studies in the Soviet Union have proven that B-15 improves heartbeats in patients with heart disease. Dr. Richard Passwater tells us, "They have also shown that vitamin B-15 quickens the healing of scar tissue and limits the side effects of heart drugs when used with it."

The most recent studies have shown that B-15 is also effective in the liver for transporting fats.

It makes blood levels of cholesterol, some other fats, and certain hormones normal again. This regulating effect is unusual because if the levels are too low, it will bring them up; if they are too high, it will lower them. B-15 also has anti-aging effects, keeping the cells alive and healthy by supplying proper amounts of oxygen to them. The recommended dosage is 150 milligrams per day.

I hope that this will encourage you to take these special vitamins to protect your heart. Of course, other substances, such as the other B complex vitamins and potassium, are also important to a healthy heart.

NATURE'S STIMULATOR

Above all, I want you to remember that walking will stimulate your whole body. It is nature's perfect body stimulator. It makes you breathe oxygen into the lungs which send rich oxygenated blood to every part of your body. It feeds every cell from your brain to your toes, and it makes your heart work. When your heart has to work, it will get stronger every day. Of course, you will do this under a doctor's care if you have a history of heart problems. Doctors are telling patients to get out and walk, run, or jog. Walk briskly, swinging the arms in rhythm, the left arm and the right leg, then the right arm and the left leg. All the vitamins in the world will not give you a strong heart without *exercise!*

REFLEXOLOGY IN CASES OF EMERGENCY

I wish that everyone would learn the few simple methods for treating heart attacks with reflex massage. It is so easy to do. Anyone, from an aged person to a very young child, can safely use the technique of reflexology when there is a sudden emergency and they are not able to use any other method to aid the victim until help arrives. Knowing how to massage the reflexes correctly might even save your own life. I have prevented several heart attacks, as have many of my students; thus patients have been saved from a badly damaged heart, or death, while waiting for the paramedics and the attention of a doctor. I am sure that many lives would be saved and that a healthy recovery rate would be much higher if everyone knew a few simple techniques of reflex massage, especially sports enthusiasts and people who like the great outdoors.

Every year, we are saddened by the high rate of deaths from heart attacks during the hunting season. People start out with such a happy anticipation of adventure away from all the confusion and pressure of city life. (Most of the people are in poor physical condition). They overindulge in alcohol, they overexert bodies that are not used to strenuous exercise, and disaster strikes. Their hearts give out and many of them never see their families again. *Don't let this happen to you!*

Check the reflex buttons to your heart to make sure that it is in good condition. Use reflex massage to strengthen and build up your heart *before* you put it to strenuous unaccustomed pressure. I will tell you how to do this later in this chapter but right now I would like you to learn to use these special methods of reflexology on yourself and also on others in case you are ever faced with an emergency heart attack. I want you to realize that the following methods are *by no means a substitute for proper medical care* but are to be used in an emergency when no help is available. They may be used in conjunction with standard medical care if it is available.

Suppose This Happens

Let us say, you are up in the mountains and you suddenly begin to feel out of breath with pains in the chest or other symptoms of heart malfunction. Because you know how to use reflex massage, *you will not panic*. You will sit down immediately. If you are too weak to dig into the reflexes in your left hand, squeeze the little finger of your left hand. See Photo 42. Hold it tightly. This should relax you enough to enable you to dig into the palm of the left hand and hunt for a sore spot. Also massage the area below the little finger. Do not let the pain of the reflex button stop you. Use whatever method is easier for you. See Photo 30. Relax! Tension causes a strain on the heart. You may have to press quite hard on the hand reflexes, or you might even use a stick, but get into those reflexes and massage hard. Massage the sore button first, then work all around it, then go back to it until the soreness eases up. If you get a twinge of pain in the left shoulder, stick your thumb into that spot and massage for a few seconds or hold a steady pressure on it, then return to massaging the reflexes in the left hand. When you feel better, you might take off your left shoe and massage the reflexes on the little toe and the pad below it. Remember that the heart is a large organ and takes up quite a large space in your chest. Since you do not know which part of the heart is malfunctioning, it is good to massage the whole area after you have massaged out most of the painful reflex buttons.

Helping Someone Else

If a person having difficulty is unable to perform reflexology on his or her own hands, I suggest that you take off his shoes and on the left foot massage the little toe and the pad below the little toe. See Diagram 8. This will probably be quite painful, but massage the whole area. As soon as you feel that you have him stabilized, go to the center of the pad in the big toe and press in hard. If it is too sore, use a lighter pressure. This can be very painful for some people. This is the reflex to the pituitary gland which will help send a flow of life energy throughout the endocrine glands. You can easily use all of these methods of reflexology on yourself if you find it necessary.

If someone else shows signs that might indicate a heart attack, you can also use the same procedure as I have told you to use on yourself. Also, to improve a failing heartbeat, use the flat section of your fist to bang on the part of the body where the head joins the neck. See Diagram 9B. This stimulates a nerve that speeds up the heartbeat.

Since we are talking of emergency treatment where there is no help available, I give you Dr. Lavitan's method of treating a severe heart attack. (He is associate editor of the *Journal of Clinical Chiropractic*.)

Massage Saves a Life

Dr. Lavitan tells us of a patient who had a heart attack right in his waiting room. It happened so quickly that by the time the doctor reached his side the victim had no pulse or blood pressure and had begun to shake all over. Death must have been seconds away. The doctor had nothing to lose, so he grabbed the man's left hand and began to really dig in and massage the palm. See Photo 30. At first, there was no reaction. Then the victim began to gasp for air. The pulse finally started up, stopped, started again, fluttered, and finally began to get into rhythm. In this case, an ambulance came and the man recovered nicely.

Vacation Saved by Reflex Massage

I was on vacation with a friend much younger than myself. We had rented a motel room on the second floor, and as we were unloading the car she grabbed a suitcase and took off up the stairs. When I got to the top I noticed her sitting on the suitcase. She was acting very strangely and was pale and sweating. She said she was dizzy, couldn't see well, was too weak to get up. I grabbed her left hand and had her hold pressure on her little finger while I pressed some of the body reflexes to the heart. I also worked on the reflexes on her head. After a few minutes she felt better and walked into the room. Because we were in a strange town, she refused to see a doctor. I made her stay in bed for the next day while I worked on the reflexes to the heart and also to the endocrine glands. We only missed one day of our vacation, and when she got home her doctor said she was okay. She was a school teacher and not used to much exercise. Overstraining the heart can be dangerous; knowing reflexology could save a life.

Another doctor's testimonial is of a woman who suffered from severe angina pains, which occurred at least once a month. They were so agonizing and came on so suddenly that she always lived in fear of the next attack. She was on regular medication including nitroglycerin, yet her medication didn't really stop the attacks or eliminate the pain. When the doctor examined her, he spent ten minutes massaging these reflexes that I have just explained to you. This happened a year and a half ago, and she hasn't had a single attack since the first treatment.

I am sure that you will agree with me that reflexology is something that everyone should learn. I hope that you never have to use this emergency information, but if you need it just once in your life, you will be glad that you knew what to do.

Relief of Heart Pains and Headaches

Dear Mildred Carter,

A church group of forty-, fifty-, and sixty-year-olds was climbing a very steep hill; we were zig-zagging our way up. Part of the way up and then again at the top, a man and woman were short of breath and were having chest pains with racing hearts. I massaged the heart reflex on the lady's left hand and told her how to do it. Then I massaged the man's heart reflex also. Both experienced immediate relief and couldn't thank me enough.

On three other occasions, headaches disappeared almost as fast. Thank you so much.

—Mrs. D. W., Registered Nurse.

REFLEXOLOGY TEST FOR POSSIBLE HEART PROBLEMS

Now let me tell you of a few simple techniques to use to make sure that your heart is in perfect condition. You should take this test a few weeks before you plan to do things that will put an extra strain on your heart—things that you are not accustomed to doing every day such as sports, hiking, shoveling snow in the winter, etc.

Earlier in this chapter, I told you of several methods for checking the reflexes for the heart. Here is another method as described by Dr. Lavitan.

Press hard on the top section of the left thumb pad. If you don't have much strength in your hands, you might use the hand massager which is described in another chapter in this book. See Photo 30. (It is wise always to have in your possession a magic reflex massager, a hand massager, a reflex comb, and a tongue probe.)

This method of reflexology can warn you of an oncoming heart attack. According to Dr. Lavitan, when you dig into the top part of the thumb pad and it hurts, it is telling you that the blood vessels going to your heart are constricting, cutting off the blood supply and reducing its oxygen. If the bottom half of the pad is where it is tender or sore, then the arteries in your heart are getting "clogged up."

If it is just a little bit sore, the possibility of a heart attack may exist but is more remote. If you should go "ouch, that really hurts" and you have to stop because it is so painful, the chances are greater that a heart attack might occur. It is much better to be forewarned of danger of a heart attack, so that you can do something to strengthen the heart immediately. Check with your chiropractor or a physician. There are many other things that could be wrong, but you have been given the warning in time to prevent an attack if you are in danger of one.

Important note: If the thumb on the right hand is also sore on these pads, you are probably not in danger of a heart attack. It is probably telling you a different story.

Dr. Lavitan says, "I particularly like this heart attack test because it's quick. It doesn't cost anything, you don't need any equipment, and you can do it yourself in fifteen seconds."

In some cases, a person will have a "diagnosed" heart condition—usually angina—and yet the left palm will not be painful. This is because many cases of angina may not be a true heart condition but simply a misplaced rib. The misplaced rib may cause muscle spasms that feel like heart pain or a heart attack. If you suspect that this might be true in your situation or that of a friend, check with a good chiropractor. (According to Dr. Lavitan, this viewpoint is shared by the eminent cardiologist, Dr. Wilfred Shute.)

The Doctor Had Given Up Hope

Dear Mrs. Carter,

My seventy-three-year-old sister took the swine flu shot. After a few days, she was taken to the hospital with a heart condition. The doctor called it heart failure. When he had given her a matter of hours to live, my other sister called me. I lived in another town thirty miles away. I called a cab and rushed to the hospital. I found her with little pulse—her heart was very weak. I gave her the reflexology heart treatment, and in less than fifteen minutes, her pulse was back to normal. She was noticing people in her room and was able to hold a conversation with me. This was on a Saturday night, and about 8:30 a.m. on Tuesday morning, her doctor released her to go home. He did not know what had made her well so quickly. Should I have told him?

—M. O.

12

How Reflexology Can Help the Stomach and Digestion

Many things can cause an upset stomach and poor digestion. Look at Diagram 12, and you will see how several factors can contribute to your discomfort. After the food goes into the stomach, it is affected by the liver and the gall bladder and then the pancreas as it passes through the small intestines on into the large intestine (colon) before it is expelled as waste.

REFLEXES TO THE STOMACH

See Diagrams 10 and 11. Notice the location of the reflex buttons to the stomach, the liver, and the gall bladder. Take the middle finger and press into the reflex button marked stomach. Is it sore? Move the finger up or down a little to find the area that is painful. See Photo 12. Usually, the stomach reflexes are quite sensitive to a little pressure. Move the finger to the right and press on the reflex buttons to the liver and the gall bladder. Then move the finger down to the small intestine reflex. Now, move the finger over and up to the colon reflexes and press here along the waistline and on several buttons on both sides of the abdomen as shown in the charts. After you have located these reflex buttons, you may use three fingers to press and hold, use the fingers on both hands simultaneously, or use the reflex roller. See Photo 15.

I have already told you how to activate these reflexes in a previous chapter, but I will repeat it here. Press and hold for the count of three, and then release for the count of three and repeat. Do this three times to each reflex. If you are having digestion problems, you must also use this same technique on the navel reflex. See Photo 11.

137

There are other less important reflexes to the stomach and other parts of the body, but to keep this simple and easy to follow I am giving you the more important ones to work on. Remember, the stomach can also be the cause of headaches.

Before I knew about reflexology, one evening my husband had a bad case of indigestion. He took every kind of anti-acid remedy that we had in the house with no relief. Finally, I suggested he take a little vinegar in water. He did this and got immediate relief.

RELIEF FROM ULCERS WITH REFLEXOLOGY

There have been many cases of ulcers relieved by reflexology. One of the main reasons is the almost immediate release from built-up nervous tension that usually is the main cause of the ulcer. The reflexes in the feet are usually the most relaxing. Just use the reflex massage method as taught earlier in this book. Next come the reflexes on the hands—search for "ouch" spots all over the hands and the feet, and when you find them, massage them for several seconds.

In all of these reflex areas, you may find it easier if you use the reflex devices described elsewhere in this book. I am speaking of the foot roller, the hand probe, and the magic massager. Also, the reflex roller is indispensable for searching out and massaging the reflexes on all parts of the body. The tongue probe is especially good for all types of stomach problems. See Photo 22.

Anyone with an ulcer or a long history of stomach problems should be under the care of a good naturopathic doctor, chiropractor, or medical doctor.

Remember, first you must get rid of stress. It is well known that a dog will not keep an ulcer if left on his own. He merely goes and lies down and relaxes and the ulcer vanishes. Can you do this? With the help of reflexology, you can!

Quiet your nerves with love for your fellow man. Anger and upset is poison in your bloodstream that goes to every cell in your body, so strive to relax. Massage the reflexes to the endocrine glands and especially the pituitary gland.

I highly recommend that you take Propolis to help cure an ulcer. Propolis is another one of nature's cures; derived from bees, it has an uncanny healing property.

Hiccups Stopped with Reflexology

When I was in Hawaii, one evening I walked into a store for something. The clerk was getting ready to close when an agitated young woman and her husband came in. She asked for an alkalizer or something similar to stop her terrible hiccups.

I told her husband to press, "Here," pointing to my stomach. He looked puzzled but walked over and pressed *my* stomach, much to my surprise! I said, "No! No! Do it to her—like this." Standing in back of her, I reached around her and pressed into her stomach with the fingers of both my hands, about halfway between the breastbone and the navel, holding about three seconds. She looked at me in pleasant surprise and said, "It is gone, the hiccups are all gone!" Her husband asked, "Are you a doctor?"

The store clerk was concerned and couldn't believe what she had witnessed. She thought I was some kind of a witch doctor.

The wonders of reflexology could be passed off as witchery or psychic healing, but it is neither of these. It is just one of nature's greatest, yet simplest, methods of natural healing.

Addicted to Reflexology

Dear Mrs. Carter:

When I was about twenty-four years of age I had five hard spots rubbed out of my intestines by a masseur friend. Since that time (I am now eighty-five years old) I have used the practice on my stomach and intestines to relieve constipation and aches and pains caused by injuries so I am addicted to the practice, also for my wife. Thank you for bringing your knowledge of body reflexology into our lives. All of your instructions are so simple and easy to follow. I am trying to register all of your instructions in my mind so I can use them on my wife and others who need natural healing.

—H. E. P.

13

How Reflexology Can Help the Colon

I am wondering how many of you realize how important the colon (large intestine) is to your general well-being and health. I was in the office of a naturopathic doctor the other day and studied some pictures of diseases and abnormalities of the colon. They were horrifying. Even I did not realize how completely the colon can become diseased, even while the body keeps on functioning. (Not comfortably, though, for sure.)

FATAL ILLNESS CAN BEGIN IN THE COLON

The colon is a good sewage system, but by neglect and abuse it becomes a cesspool. It can be the cause of more physical human misery and suffering, mental and moral, than any other known source.

The colon takes up a large space in your body. It carries off all of the waste matter that is left from the food and drink that you send into your stomach by way of the mouth.

What happens when you don't empty your garbage can for a few days? What if you emptied just part of the garbage? What would happen to the garbage that didn't get emptied for months, yes, even years, as you kept adding to the waste? You can buy a new garbage can every so often, but do you want to have to buy a new colon? Some people have to, you know! If you could have seen the pictures of the insides of some diseased colons, as I did, you wouldn't let one day go by before you started to do something about helping your colon to maintain or regain its normal health.

TROUBLES OF THE COLON

Notice the colon in Diagram 13. See how large it is and how much of the body it occupies. Can you picture the whole inside of this organ literally covered with sores, all inflamed and abscessed and unable to carry off the waste material that you are still forcing into it? No wonder there is such a high rate of colon cancer today.

While your colon is filled with pollution, your bloodstream is drawing some of this poison and feeding it back into the body.

Remember that *every cell of the body is served by the blood*. It nourishes the cells, replaces "worn out" parts, and carries away waste products. If you have an infection in the body, such as infected teeth, the doctors fear it will poison the rest of your body, in some way causing arthritis or other related diseases. How many of you are letting your blood feed your body on decayed sewage from your colon? Do not wait until it is too late! Start to repair it now with reflex massage. I will also tell you of other remedies to heal a sick colon if it is not completely beyond repair.

After studying pictures of diseased colons, I asked a doctor, "How can people live with such terrible colons?" He said, "The body is a wonderful system beyond our understanding and is able to do marvelous jobs repairing itself."

USING REFLEX MASSAGE FOR THE COLON

First let us try a little test to see if the colon reflexes are tender or sore. Since we are just testing, let us try the colon reflexes on the hand. The colon reflex is almost straight across the middle of the hand. See Diagram 6.

Take the thumb of the right hand or a massaging device and start pressing it into the pad in the middle of the left hand. See Photos 33 and 36. Starting below the pad under the little finger, search for tender spots as you work the thumb or a massaging device across the center of the palm until you come to the area between the thumb and the forefinger. If you find a tender reflex on your way across the palm, massage it for a moment or hold pressure on it to the count of seven.

Change hands, and with the thumb of the left hand, press and massage across the center of the palm of the right hand as you search out tender spots that indicate malfunction elsewhere in the body. This does not necessarily mean that it is only the colon reflexes that are giving you the warning signal, for there are several reflexes crowded into the palms of the hands.

Go on to the reflexes in the pad below the thumb. This area also has reflexes to several other parts of the body, so if it has any tender spots in it, be sure to massage them out. In many cases, a reflex device will probably be helpful here, especially the magic reflex massager.

Go to the web between the thumb and forefinger. Using the thumb and forefinger of the right hand or a reflex device, pinch and massage this web on the left hand. See Photos 37 and 38. This is another area that holds reflexes to several parts of the body, so if there are any tender spots, be sure to massage every one of them out. Remember that we must have the whole body in harmony in order to bring it into perfect balance and health.

Change hands and massage the web of the right hand. Never do one side of the body without doing the other. This would cause an unbalanced condition of the whole electrical nervous system.

We are going to massage another area where the reflexes also go to many parts of the body. From the web that you have just been massaging, press the thumb on up into the fleshy part of the hand between the bones of the thumb and the forefinger. See Diagrams 9A and D. In this area, search for tender reflexes in the center and also along the bones of the thumb and the forefinger. In other chapters, you will be referred to this same reflex area for various ailments.

Other Colon Reflexes

Now, we will go to the forefinger for another reflex to the colon. Press the finger starting at the nail, searching for a tender reflex. Work all the way up the arm as in Photo 43. There is also a reflex to the colon just under the lower lip.

I do not want to give you too many reflex points to work on as it gets confusing when there are too many to remember. Since the function of this organ is so important to the well-being of the whole body, I want you to do everything that you can to get it into as perfect condition as possible and then keep it that way.

Massaging the Feet

Now, we will go to the colon reflexes in the feet. If it is difficult to lift your foot high enough to work on it, I suggest the reflex foot massager. See Photos 44 and 45. It is perfect for massaging all the reflexes on the bottom of the feet, especially the reflex to the colon. I use this reflex massager quite often while watching television in the evening. It keeps my body in perfect order while it relaxes the nervous system. Don't use it for too long at a time at first.

For those of you who have your feet up where you can work on them: With your thumb or a reflex device, start at the center or waistline of the foot. See Diagram 8 and Photos 46 and 47. Using a pressing, rolling motion, go across the foot toward the reflexes to the spine, then continue to massage on down the inside of the spine reflexes, all the time searching for tender reflexes. When you find tender areas, either hold a steady pressure on them or massage them. If you are having trouble with the colon, you will find some of these spots almost too sore to touch. Start out gently at first, and as the soreness becomes less, you can increase the pressure.

Massage in this manner on both feet. Massage down the outer side of the foot toward the heel. You cannot be sure if it is the colon or other organs sending out the pain signal as you massage over certain areas. Don't let this concern you. Just keep in mind that where congestion exists, disease will result, so massage it out.

OTHER REMEDIES FOR THE COLON

Since the colon is one of the most important organs in your body, I will tell you a few more things to do along with the reflexology treatments to keep it healthy.

The most common disease of the colon, diverticulosis, strikes one of every three people over sixty. Before 1900, this disease was almost unknown. Then diets were rich in whole grains, fruits, and vegetables, all good sources of fiber. Fiber, the indigestible portion of food, passes unaltered into the lower bowel, adding bulk to the stool and helping keep the bowels in good working order. We hear much today about bran, for instance. One of the best sources of bran fiber is the husk of wheat and other grains. White flour, meat, dairy products, and sugar are low in fiber. Low-fiber diets create small, hard stools. When these reach the colon, that organ has to clamp down and squeeze unnaturally hard to force them through. A lifetime of this kind of overwork weakens the muscles of the colon, causing small pouches to protrude out the lining wall of the colon. These pouches are called diverticula; if they are present, you have diverticulosis. When bran fiber was added to the diet of those suffering from this malfunction of the colon, 90 percent of the patients were relieved of the disease. Also relieved were such symptoms as bloody stools, constipation, and nausea.

Do you understand why I give you this advice along with the reflexology massage? Things of nature work together to create a perfect balance, and fiber is one of nature's healing foods. We might refer to it as a scrub brush as it passes through the alimentary canal. See Diagram 12.

SAUERKRAUT—A HEALING AGENT

Sauerkraut is a health-giving, vitamin-producing food that has been a boon to man for centuries. Sauerkraut regulates the digestive processes, overcomes vitamin and mineral deficiencies, and stimulates the body to longer life. It provides the body with all of the benefits of green and leafy vegetables at all times of the year besides adding other qualities which other vegetables do not have.

Sauerkraut supplies lime, iron, bone and blood builders, and other vital vitamins and minerals. It is a fermented product made from cabbage. To certain peoples of the world, sauerkraut means health and an extraordinary sense of well-being; it is an economical and satisfying food. It is an easily digestible vegetable that combines, in a most savory manner, with other foods and—by the experience of many centuries—also is a food that seems to prolong life.

You may wonder why I am writing so much about sauerkraut in this chapter on the colon. It is a perfect food to help heal problems in the colon. I know of no other natural food that can take its place.

It is a proven fact that some ailments are caused by the large amounts of harmful bacteria that reside in the large intestine. These intestinal microbes manufacture poisons that spread throughout the body. These microbes are produced by the waste products of the food we eat.

According to Metchnikoff of the Pasteur Institute, "In arteriosclerosis [hardening of the arteries] in the cases of patients who do not suffer from special diagnosed causes, the blame must fall on the innumerable microbes that swarm in our intestines and poison us."

Metchnikoff claimed that, "The presence of large numbers of lactic acid bacilli will interfere with the development of the putrefactive bacteria."

How Sauerkraut Helps

This is the role that sauerkraut plays in helping your colon heal itself: It is a natural lactic acid food that overcomes harmful germs in the large intestines (used in place of dangerous drugs) and it helps relieve constipation, which is largely the cause of colon problems. Sauerkraut is an excellent regulator and a natural laxative.

A Friend Is Helped

A friend of mine said that she had to give up square dancing because of colon problems. I said, "Why don't you take sauerkraut? She was surprised at my suggestion, but she did say she would try it. (She wouldn't try reflexology as she couldn't understand how it works.) I didn't see her for several months after that. I went back to the dance one night and she came up to me and thanked me for making her well. I had forgotten the earlier incident, so I didn't know what she was talking about. I thought she was talking about reflexology, but then she began to explain to me about taking the sauerkraut. She had eaten sauerkraut every day; her colon had gotten well, and she had been dancing every night since.

Sauerkraut Helps Many Organs

It is not only because of its varied vitamin content that I recommend sauerkraut in the diet, but also because it is rich in mineral substances. It contains large quantities of calcium, sulfur, chlorine, and iodine in a natural form.

Because of its minerals, sauerkraut is a valuable aid in the preservation of teeth, gums, hair, and bones. We know that sauerkraut acts as a blood cleanser and relieves constipation. It also aids the function of the kidneys and the bladder and is a helpful agent in cases of functional heart trouble.

Try to include sauerkraut in your menu every day. It is good cooked with pork and garlic. It makes a delicious dressing combined with apples and onions and stuffed in a duck or a chicken. It is good to use in salads, cold or heated, with oil and garlic powder added. If it is too sour for you, add honey to taste. Eat applesauce with sauerkraut; it is delicious. Drink the sauerkraut juice to help in a reducing diet. I would suggest a daily intake of sauerkraut or juice as a preventive measure against general ill health.

ENEMAS FOR PROBLEMS IN THE COLON

Some doctors advise us to take enemas; others advise us not to take enemas. Here we are going to tell you how to take enemas to help a sick colon, and we are going to use one of our wonder foods, *blackstrap molasses*. Yes! An enema taken with this black magic has cured abscess in the colon. I know this is true because it was my colon that was healed. This was in the days before I knew very much about natural healing. I knew for a long time that I had an abscess in my colon. It would become very painful at times, and sometimes it would break and drain. I never went to doctors unless I was having a baby. They always wanted to operate on me for something when I did go, so I quit going. I continually studied natural healing methods and got a small book about blackstrap molasses. It said to use two tablespoons of the molasses to a quart of water for an enema, so I started to take the enemas and felt better almost immediately. Soon the abscess started to drain; it looked like a boil draining with pus and blood. I kept taking the molasses enemas for a few more days, and I never had any trouble with the colon again.

The Key to Locked Bowels

Mrs. A. tells of a day a few years back when she became very constipated. A doctor told her that she had "locked bowels" and that they would have to operate. She called her sister, who was a nurse, and told her what the doctor had said. "Don't you do anything until I get there," the sister told her. When her sister arrived the next day, she asked for some blackstrap molasses. (This should be from a health food store only.) She prepared an enema with it, making it quite strong. She gave her sister the enemas, one after another, until she finally got the bowel to release the blockage, and her sister was saved from a dangerous operation. Mrs. A. claims that blackstrap molasses and her sister saved her life.

One day, I was visiting a chiropractor who was always interested in talking about health. We would go into his office and talk for hours. I have learned many things from this wonderful man who was interested in all types of natural healings. He told me of the time that he worked in a clinic that specialized in colon diseases. They had a special formula that they used on all colon patients to cure problems of the colon without operations. I am giving this formula to you as I have given it to a few others who have had success with it. Keep in mind that if you do not get results in a few days from any of the methods that I have given you, see a doctor—a good naturopath, if possible.

FORMULA FOR A SICK COLON

2 oz. chlorophyll, liquid or powder
1 tablespoon glycerine
1 teaspoon Golden Seal (liquid tincture, if available)
4 oz. witch hazel,
8 oz. stale beer (12 hours old)

Mix all ingredients and use as an enema. Retain or hold this enema one half-hour. Do this at least once a day or more often for two days. If your problem is severe, extend the treatment to five or six days. Then take the enemas every other day. Take orally: acidophilus, yogurt, and sauerkraut every day.

What to Eat to Keep Your Colon Healthy

It has been proven in clinical tests that the people who used a lot of the cabbage family in their diets had much more freedom from all diseases of the colon than those who ate none or very little of the cabbage plants. These include broccoli, brussels sprouts, and cauliflower. If you are inclined to have colon problems, start including these good-for-you vegetables in your diet. Remember, especially, sauerkraut is included as one of these colon-healing vegetables.

14

How to Use Reflex Massage
to Relieve Back Pain

All practitioners recognize the importance that the spine has in the general health of the whole body. A great part of one's well-being depends on the condition of the spine. The largest percentage of back pain is caused from tension in the muscles that surround the spine. When undue strain is placed on a muscle somewhere in the back area, it tends to tighten and pull on certain vertebrae, causing the spine to be pulled out of alignment. We are all aware that the body can never function in perfect health if the spine is out of alignment.

LOW BACK PAIN IS THE LARGEST SINGLE
MEDICAL COMPLAINT IN THE UNITED STATES

Many people in our country have suffered from this painful malady for years. They have gone to doctors and chiropractors without any lasting relief. When they finally searched out a reflexologist who understood the method of massaging the reflexes, in most cases they found permanent relief.

Back Pain Relieved All Over the World

I have received hundreds of letters from all over the world telling of the wonderful relief people have received from painful back problems. They used the simple but rewarding method of massaging the reflexes to the back that are located on their hands and on their feet. Now we will go a step further and show you how to use this wonderful healing method of massaging reflexes on other parts of the body, which will also bring almost instant relief from back pain.

148

Back Helped for Good

Dear Mrs. Carter,

I was troubled with painful back muscles for several weeks. Nothing seemed to help for long. One day, I decided I would try a different technique of reflex massage, since it had always helped me for other painful symptoms. I checked my hand with the chart and decided that I had not been massaging in the correct place. The muscles on the right side of my back were affected, so I felt for tender spots on the pad of my right hand below the little finger, and sure enough, I discovered some very tender places. After rubbing them a few minutes, the pain in my back lessened. In three days, all pain and tightness were gone and never returned. It pays to use your own testing along with the help of the charts when a problem doesn't clear up with ordinary directions. I truly believe that there is a reflex someplace that will alleviate pain and eliminate its cause, if we just search for it. I have proved this to be true. Thank you.

—Mrs. J. S.

HOW TO MASSAGE THE TENDER BUTTONS

Let me explain about using the reflexes in the hands and the feet to relieve many types of back pain.

You will note in Diagram 8 that the whole spinal column is located in the exact center of the body. Now, look to the feet and note that from the big toe on the inside of the foot there is almost a replica of the spine. Follow this area with the fingers or a reflex device as it progresses along the foot to the heel. If you have any weakness in the spine, you will find very tender spots along this area. If the tenderness is near the toe, then the spine is weak between the shoulders. As it progresses toward the heel, you are following the spine down to the tail bone (coccyx). When you massage any of these tender places, you are stimulating a renewed life force into the part of the spine that for some reason is not getting a full supply of energy. When you massage these tender buttons on your feet, it is like turning on an electric circuit that has been cut off from its source of power. See Diagram 8.

In the hands we find the same reflexes to the spine, but our blueprint of the electrical circuit of reflex buttons is moved to the forefinger and the bone that goes from the base of the finger to the wrist. See Photo 48. We also massage the bony structures of the thumb where it joins the wrist. This helps the lower back.

Cure in a Few Minutes

Dear Mrs. Carter,

When my brother brought me to you, I was in so much pain from my back I could hardly walk. I had strained my lower back about a week before, and it kept getting worse instead of better. My family finally talked me into going to see you. In just a few minutes my pain was gone after you pressed a few reflexes in my back and then on the backs of my legs. Now any time I have a backache, I have my wife work on these reflexes like you showed us. We can't thank you enough.

—S. M.

WHY OTHER TREATMENTS SOMETIMES FAIL

When muscles are not loose and pliable, they can pull the bones out of place again (after a spinal adjustment) if they remain tight. In most cases, chiropractic adjustment helps, but if the back does not respond to adjustment, turn to reflex massage to relax and loosen up those tight muscles.

All muscles need fresh oxygenated blood and can't respond to nerve impulses without it. Tight muscles are starved for oxygen. So, let us first learn to loosen those muscles. When you massage the muscles to loosen them so that fresh oxygenated blood can flow into them, you are also reopening channels for the flow of life energy to the electrical system. The life force once more flows through all of the circuits and bring nature's healing power into play. When you press on certain reflex buttons, you open channels through which the healing forces surge to malfunctioning areas of the body.

MOST CONVENTIONAL TREATMENTS ARE USELESS

When you consider the importance of keeping the muscles pliable and strong, you will understand the harm most conventional methods can cause. A back brace causes muscles to become stiff from lack of normal movement, and traction does not give permanent relief because it doesn't relieve tight muscles. When muscles become too tight over a period of time, they lose circulation, and without adequate blood supply they deteriorate. Drug therapy does nothing for tight hamstring muscles. Then, there is surgery! Even after the expense and suffering, there is still no guarantee that the pain will not return or that you will not become crippled.

Why not try loosening up the tight muscles before you turn to any of these symptomatic treatments? Give reflex massage a chance. Remember, when you are massaging these muscles, to dig in deep with the fingers and rub *across* the muscles, not with them. Loosen them up so that the life force can circulate through them naturally.

Son-in-Law Cured of Low Back Pain

I was visiting my daughter and family not long ago. My son-in-law had been suffering from a back injury for several months. When I visited them, I would give him reflexology treatment and relieve him for the time I was there. They would never follow through with the treatments after I left, so his old problem would return. The last time I visited them, I had him lie on the floor so that I could test the hamstring muscles on the back of the thighs. These were very tight and hard and were painful when massaged. After I loosened up those muscles, his back was free from pain, and he slept like a baby all night.

LOW BACK PAIN IS CAUSED BY TIGHT MUSCLES IN THE HAMSTRINGS

When the hamstring muscles in the backs of the legs become tight, they pull on the pelvis. You can see how this in turn pulls on all the muscles and tendons of the lower back. This places pressure on the spine and throws the back out of alignment, causing the discs to slip, rupture, or disintegrate.

Let us now learn how to massage these hamstring muscles to loosen them up and get the oxygenated blood flowing back through them. Sit on the edge of a chair, preferably a straight, hard chair. Relax one leg and place the fingers on the muscles of the thigh on the back of the leg. Press and pull the fingers across the muscles with one hand, then the other. Use the fingers of the other hand to pull across in the opposite direction. Do you feel any hard muscles? Dig in deeper and deeper as you search for a hard, bound muscle. Start at the buttocks and press and pull all the way to where the muscles end at the knee. When you find a hard, tight muscle, massage, press, and pull it. Remember, you are to pull the fingers *across* the muscle, not with it.

When you have finished with this leg, do the same massage on the other one. Remember, if you find any hard, tight muscles in this area, they must be worked out and become soft and pliable when relaxed. Your trouble may be caused by hard tight muscles lying very deep, even those next to the bone, so don't be afraid to massage deep. Work every tight area that you find. It could be quite painful in some cases at first.

If you have someone else to massage the hamstring muscles for you, then lie on a hard table or even the floor. After you get the muscles back to normal, you will find that the reflexes to the back will respond much more quickly, and you will get even better results than you had previously.

Feet Can Cause Back Problems

Some 20 percent of back pain is caused by flat feet. It can be corrected by wearing corrective shoes along with reflex massage. Experiment by wearing different shoes. Many times shoes are the cause of backaches.

Walking Is Beneficial to the Back

Walking is the best exercise for any back problems; it is nature's method of strengthening all of the muscles in your body, especially your back muscles. It sends more blood and oxygen to every cell and tissue in your body, including the brain, eyes, and all internal organs. You may walk briskly, but there is no need to run. Jogging has proved to be harmful to 40 percent of those who jog.

A rebounder, which is a small trampoline, will prove to be very beneficial without harming the bone structure of the body and will give you many more benefits than jogging. Vitamin C has been proven to help many a backache.

15

How Reflexology Can Strengthen the Liver

The liver is the largest gland in the body. It weighs about three pounds in an adult and has, at all times, about one-quarter of all the blood in the body circulating through it.

The liver performs many tasks: it is a great filter and it is a natural antiseptic and purgative device. It manufactures bile, which the intestines use to digest fats and prevent constipation. It helps to supply some of the substances for making blood and it also stores sugar within itself.

HAND AND FOOT MASSAGE

Since the liver is such a large organ, you will massage a larger area than usual. The reflexes to the liver are on the right hand and the right foot. Place the thumb of the left hand on the pad of the right hand or foot just below the little finger or little toe. See Diagrams 6 and 8. Press and roll this area searching for tender spots. When you find them, massage them for about ten counts. In many cases, you will probably need a reflex device like the magic massager or the hand massager. The liver is sometimes stubborn in its response to healing methods. Be persistent in your efforts to open up the channels to allow the electric life forces to surge in full power to the ailing liver.

HOW THE LIVER RESISTS

Though the liver sometimes seems to resist our efforts to help bring it back to its natural full capacity of work, it is one gland that can replace parts of itself. Remember its importance to your complete health, and massage all of the reflexes to the liver.

153

If you have a very sluggish liver, start out with a light massage the first few times. You can expect different reactions from this treatment of the liver. If it is very sensitive and you do have a severe reaction, don't massage the liver reflexes for a few days. Give nature a chance to throw off excess poisons and adjust itself to the increased circulation that the electrical life force has put into motion.

There is also a very important liver reflex on the large pad of the right thumb, and one on the right big toe as well. This is the same area that you worked when you worked on the reflex to the heart on the left hand and foot. Massage this pad very thoroughly, and if you find tender reflexes here, remember our motto, "If it hurts, massage it out."

Go to the web between the thumb and the forefinger. Pinch and squeeze the reflexes in this area. If you find any tender spots, massage them out. Remember that they also open up the electrical channels to other parts of the body. See Photos 37 and 38.

While you are on the web, with the thumb on top of the hand, work the thumb right up between the bones of the thumb and the forefinger. See Diagram 9D. Press and squeeze this whole area. If it is easier for you to use the forefinger on the top of the hand instead of the thumb, then do it that way. Massage along the bones on both sides as you search for tender spots.

LIVER REFLEXES ALSO HELP THE GALLBLADDER

The gallbladder is lodged on the under surface of the right lobe of the liver. It is a pear-shaped vibro-muscular receptacle for the bile. This is also the receptacle where the very painful hardened masses called gallstones are found. I have received letters from many people telling me of how reflex massage on the hands and feet has dissipated gallstones after a few treatments. It is not known whether the treatments so relaxed the gall duct that they passed off or whether the stones dissolved. If you find any of these reflex buttons to be tender, massage them until all soreness is gone. Do not try to rub out all of the tenderness at one time. Give nature time to relieve this congestion. Remember, it took a long time for the body to get into this condition, so give it time to perform its own miracle of healing. The channels of the electrical life forces are opened when you press and massage these special reflex buttons to the liver and gallbladder.

Location of the Gallbladder Reflexes

Notice on Diagrams 10 and 11 that the reflex buttons to the liver are just below the ribs on the right side, and the gallbladder reflexes are located just below these buttons. With your middle finger, gently press in this area. Both fingers may be used simultaneously once you have located the reflex buttons. Remember that the liver covers a large area and you may find more than one "ouch" button. Hold a steady pressure on any tender reflex button that you find. Start just at the right of the navel and gently press, working over to your right side. Hold each tender reflex gently to the count of seven.

Now use the method described earlier in this book: Lay your hand flat on this whole area and in a clockwise motion roll the hand about three times over the whole right side. With all five fingers pressed together, place one or both hands just under the rib cage and vibrate or jiggle them. Continue this vibration until you have covered the whole liver area. With the flat of the right hand or both hands, lightly tap the whole liver area. Tapping with a wire brush here also will give you a feeling of renewed energy and health. The metal in the teeth of the brush adds to the power of the electrical energy.

HEAD REFLEXES TO THE LIVER

If you want to further stimulate the liver, look at Diagram 2 to see the reflexes to the liver located on the top of the head. Use pressure on each of these, holding to a slow count of about three. These will also be stimulated when you use the tapping method with the fingers or the wire brush as shown in Photos 2 and 3.

Now we turn to the reflexes in the ears. The ears contain reflexes to the whole body. Since it is difficult to pinpoint each reflex in such a small area, just massage the whole ear, searching for special "ouch" spots. Whatever this tender reflex is connected to, it is giving you a cry for help, so give it a few moments of massage by pinching and pulling on the whole ear. See Diagram 15 and Photos 18, 19, and 20.

16

How Reflexology Can Help
the Pancreas and the Spleen

HELPING THE PANCREAS

The pancreas is one of the major balancing mechanisms of your metabolism. This is the maker of insulin that lowers the sugar in the bloodstream (while adrenalin from your adrenal glands raises it).

I want to give you a warning—if you have diabetes, you often induce an increase in the supply of insulin when you massage the reflexes to the pancreas. Several times I have had people come to me after a treatment to ask if reflex massage could make a change in the insulin they need. One man said he had to cut his insulin by fifty percent after taking two treatments.

The pancreas lies just below the stomach. See Diagrams 10, 12, and 13. Study Diagram 10 to find a reflex button on the left side of the body. When you are massaging the reflexes to the pancreas, use the push-button method by pressing with the middle finger or all fingers. Starting on the left side below the ribs, press and hold for three seconds. Then, move an inch toward the center of the body and press again. Follow this procedure across the body to a little above the navel. If you find an "ouch" spot, press and hold it several times.

In Diagram 2, notice that there are reflex buttons near the outer edges on the top of the head. Press these areas to see if there is tenderness. You will probably stimulate these reflexes as you go over the head with the fists and the wire brush as explained in the chapter on reflexes in the head, but test them out anyway.

A Facial Reflex

While you are looking at Diagram 2, notice the reflex button just above the lip. Test this for tenderness also. See Photo 49.

Reflexes in Hands and Feet

I cannot tell you often enough of the importance of the reflexes located in the hands and the feet. Many illnesses have been overcome by no other method than massaging the reflexes in the feet and the hands. Pain from most causes has been stopped within seconds by pressing certain reflex buttons located in these areas.

Look at Diagram 5 to see how the reflexes to the pancreas are located across the foot. Use the thumb, or the reflex roller if it is easier for you, to massage clear across the left foot and part way across the right foot. See Photos 44 and 45. As you massage the pancreas reflexes, you will be covering the reflexes to several other glands as well. If you find this particular area of the pancreas especially tender, massage it out.

The above also holds true for the reflexes in the hands. Use the same technique to massage the reflexes to the pancreas by massaging across the left hand and also the right hand as you did on the feet. As you can see in Diagram 6, the reflexes in the hands are crowded one on top of the other. As you massage in this area, you are sending a charge of electrical healing force to many organs and glands in the body that are far removed from the area being massaged. This is why the magic massager gets such fantastic results when used conscientiously.

HELPING THE SPLEEN

Now let us look at the spleen. Notice in Diagram 13 that the spleen is located over part of the pancreas. The reflex to this little gland is just under or below the pad of the little toe near the heart reflex on the left foot and also on the left hand just below the pad of the little finger. See Diagrams 6 and 8.

Use the same technique to massage these reflexes as you did for the pancreas. If you find an "ouch" spot in this reflex to the spleen, you might be anemic. This will give you a warning to have your blood checked. Anemia is caused by lack of iron in the blood and can cause serious trouble if neglected for a long period of time. You may also need folic acid. By massaging this reflex to the spleen, you will be opening up channels allowing the electric force to bring natural health into the spleen.

17

Reflexology to Help Ailing Kidneys and Bladder

HELPING THE KIDNEYS

The kidney is another important organ of the body. When the kidneys fail to function, the body also stops functioning, so we can see that it is very important to keep the kidneys at top performance at all times. In this day of poisoned air, poisoned foods, and poisoned water, the kidneys have a very heavy work load trying to filter out all these toxins.

I have had friends die within a few days after being taken to the hospital for kidney problems. The doctors began to administer large doses of antibiotics and other drugs to fight off infections. The kidneys began to malfunction in the first place because they could not handle the impurities of the body; then, when they were flooded with massive doses of toxic poisons, they just collapsed.

Testing Kidney Reflexes

Notice in Diagram 8 that the kidney reflexes are located just a little above the center line, near the middle of the foot. Press on this reflex. If it is tender, you will know there is not enough circulation of the energy life force going to the kidneys. Massage this area a few times. It may be very tender. If you have thick soles or calluses on your feet, you may need a reflex device such as the little hand reflex massager. The roller massager and also the foot massager work well here. See Photo 50. When massaging the reflexes to the kidneys, use caution and do not massage them very long at a time, not over thirty seconds at first. Remember, when you massage all of the reflexes, you are releasing a lot of poison into the system and the kidneys have to work harder to get rid of it. So give them just a little help in the beginning.

Now look to the hands. On Diagram 6 see where the reflexes are located in the center of the hands. Press and massage the kidney reflexes in the hands as you did on the feet. See Photos 33 and 36. When you use the magic reflex massager (Photo 51), you will naturally massage the kidney reflexes as you press the little fingers of the magic massager into all of the reflexes in the hands. Placing clamps on the thumb and first two fingers will help kidneys and bladder. See Photo 52.

Body Reflexes for the Kidneys

Remember, malfunction of the kidneys affects the bladder and sex glands, so when you massage the reflexes to the kidneys, you also activate the sex glands and bladder. See in Diagrams 10 and 11 that the kidney reflexes are near the sides of the body. With the fingers, press into this area, which is in the soft space between the rib cage and the hip bone. This position will place your thumbs on the soft area of the back. Now, slide the thumbs a little more toward the spine, feeling for tender spots. This is about where your kidneys are located. Press and hold for the count of three, release for three counts, then repeat three times. Do not press hard, just hold with a light pressure, but hard enough to feel the pressure. Now massage the kidney reflexes located on the head (Diagram 2). Remember, kidney problems can cause weak eyes.

When you do a complete body massage, you will be stimulating the reflexes to the kidneys as well as the reflexes to the bladder and sex glands. See Photos 19, 47, and 53 for methods of stimulating healing energy in the whole body.

Faulty kidneys can lead to serious illnesses, so if you still have problems with your kidneys after a few days of reflex massage, you had better go to your naturopathic doctor. If a medical doctor is needed, he or she will advise you.

HELP FOR THE BLADDER

The main function of the bladder is to store urine for periodic release. It changes position and shape according to fullness. It is composed of a smooth muscle coat like that of the intestine but of greater thickness. Each kidney empties into a ureter, which then empties into the bladder. The bladder empties into the urethra, which conducts the urine from the bladder to the exterior.

On the inside of the foot, almost next to the pad of the heel, is a soft spongy area. See Diagram 8. You will find the reflexes in this area very tender if you are having any problems with the bladder. Using the thumb, massage any part that is tender with a gentle circular motion. Be sure to massage these reflexes on both feet. These reflexes are so near the location of the reflexes to the rectum, prostate, and lower spine that you will probably not be able to tell the difference as you massage the tenderness out. Remember, if it hurts, massage it out, because something in this area is not getting enough electrical life force to enable it to heal itself. You may also use heel pad massage to help the bladder. Just grab the heel pad in the hand and dig the fingers under it as shown in Photo 47. Always do the reflexes on both feet.

Using Hand Reflexes

Let us go to the hand reflexes for the bladder, in the web of the hand between the thumb and the forefinger. You will find reflexes to many parts of the body here, including the reflex to the bladder. If you find an "ouch" spot, either in the palm of the hand or on the back or top side, then massage it out.

Many types of bladder problems have been relieved by using these reflex techniques on the hands and the feet. These reflexes are very powerful in helping the body heal itself.

As you massage the bladder reflexes on the feet, continue massaging on up the bottom of the foot to the center where the kidney reflex is located. Use this same technique as you massage the bladder reflexes in the hands. Massage from the soft area in front of the thumb on the palm of the hand and follow the reflexes to the ureters right up to the kidney reflexes in the center of the hand. Always do this massage to both hands and feet unless you are told differently. Now, let us pinch and massage the reflexes in the backs of the legs as we did the reflexes for hemorrhoids and prostate. No wonder these reflexes hurt so badly when massaged; they are related to so many parts of our lower extremities.

You will also massage the reflexes in the wrists, but instead of pinching cords, you will press and massage all areas of the wrist, searching out any tender buttons that you might find. This is to be done on the entire wrist, front and back. See Photo 40.

Using Head and Body Reflexes

When you follow the directions for stimulating the reflexes in the head, you will naturally be activating the reflexes to all of these organs and glands. See Diagram 2 and Photos 2, 3, 4, and 54.

Look at Diagrams 6, 10, and 11 to see where the bladder is located. Just above the pubic bone is a soft spongy area. Take the fingers of both hands and press in gently. You will be pressing on the bladder. Do not use a massaging motion here, but hold a steady pressure for a slow count of three, then release and count to three again. Do this three times. Now, place the palm of the right hand on this bladder area and place the palm of the left hand on top of the right hand and hold for a few moments. It will be best to do this on bare skin. If another person can do this for you, he or she will be sending an even stronger force of healing energy from the energy in his or her own body. This holds true for most of the reflex massages.

PROTEIN RELATED TO KIDNEY STONES

Too much protein in your diet can lead to kidney stones, a painful condition that afflicts an estimated one million Americans, according to a leading medical researcher.

Dr. Helen Linkswiler, a nutritionist at the University of Wisconsin, Madison, gave nine different combinations of purified protein and calcium supplements to fifteen male and female adult volunteers. She found that those volunteers who received high levels of protein lost calcium from their bodies even when they received calcium supplements. Lost calcium was excreted through the kidneys, where it could build up to form kidney stones, she explained.

Dr. Linkswiler has stated that her data show that high protein levels can be devastating to the bones. She believes that if we lost as much calcium as the volunteers did, 60 mg per day over a period of ten years, we would essentially have lost 10 to 25 percent of our body's calcium, 99 percent of which comes from our bones.

She added that those who received low levels of dietary protein did not lose calcium. People who took 25 grams of protein a day— about average for American adults—lost only a small amount.

Dr. Linkswiler advised that patients with kidneys stones be treated by reducing their protein intake rather than restricting calcium.

18

Reflexology and the Sex Glands (Gonads)

The sex glands are very important glands. These glands of reproduction are the easiest glands to regenerate back to health. No one knows the suffering that can be caused by the malfunctioning of these reproduction organs unless they have experienced such an ailment.

There have been too many unnecessary operations to remove these organs in women. In men, doctors operate to remove the prostate when natural methods of healing would have helped these organs return to health.

I have cured many cases of "female trouble" in women and malfunctioning of the prostate in men with the magic healing power of reflex massage. Infertility and impotency in women and men have been overcome by the simple method of pressing and massaging certain reflex buttons. I have a letter from one of my students telling me of several cases in which she has helped to overcome impotency.

How Reflexology Overcame a Man's Impotency

Dear Mildred Carter,

I had been giving reflexology treatments to an elderly couple for some time when they said they wanted to talk to me about a personal matter. It was embarrassing for them to tell me that the man was completely impotent. They wanted to know if reflexology could help. I assured them that it could and went to work on the certain reflexes to stimulate the man's gonads (sex glands).

I was a little surprised when they told me on their next visit that the treatment had worked and they were as happy as newlyweds. The wife had tears in her eyes as she thanked me and said they had always had a happy life together until he became impotent. Now their happiness was complete once more.

—A Student

We all know that a normal sex life is important to health. If our organs of reproduction are diseased and malfunctioning, we cannot enjoy normal, satisfactory sex experiences. I am glad that we can now talk openly about sex without the embarrassment that used to go with the subject.

I do not think that sexual freedom is the answer. I feel that the sex act was given to us as a beautiful sacred gift for reproduction and was never meant to be used for a sensation of cheap pleasure of the moment. Animals do not misuse sex.

Many doctors are in disagreement on the subject of the freedom of sex. They are all in agreement that sex is necessary to keep the body healthy when used as it was meant to be used, with *love*. But many feel as I do, that free sex is leading to the degeneration of the nation and especially our young people.

When some people tell us there is no such thing as morality, they might look at history and learn why so many nations fell. I am not a moralist; I only study facts and results.

SEX IS IMPORTANT TO BEAUTY

Sex is one of the strongest drives in the animal world, and in man it has a more important function than to create new life. All of the endocrine glands are interrelated; when the sex urge begins to diminish, it is a sure sign of the slowing down of one or more glands that are directly responsible for the health and well-being of the body. Reflexology can stimulate the endocrine glands and retard the progress of aging.

People with a strong sex drive have radiant and magnetic personalities. They attract others and keep their affection. Self-reliance, self-assurance, luminosity, and sparkling eyes are indications of healthy sex glands.

Sexual repression often results in extreme cruelty, sadism, and other abnormalities.

To make sex meaningful, it must remain an integral part of our moral character, and the physical expression of love through sex should be a sacred ritual.

Male and female sexual intercourse brings polarization to *balanced* mates. It is a great vitalizing force for both when true love creates sexual desire. The scientific explanation of the multiplied power of sex lies in the fact that not only the bodies of men and women but also their thinking becomes polarized. This polarization can only come from sex mating between man and woman. That is why homosexuality has a weakening effect rather than a strengthening one. When a male has sexual relations with another male, or a female with a female, there is not a polarization, but rather a depolarization, which has a devitalizing effect.

Nature will not tolerate any violation of sex balance whatsoever. That is why we see anguish, disease, frustrations, divorces, bankruptcies, and many forms of unhappiness around us everywhere in small scale; and hatreds, enmities, and wars in large scale. All of the troubles of all the world lie in that one cause—breach of the law of polarity which upsets the balance of every transaction between *divided pairs*. When a transaction between divided pairs fails to *unite* those divided pairs, unhappiness is as sure to follow as night follows day.

THE IMPORTANCE OF LOVE

All living things respond to love. Flowers, animals, trees, and birds are like humans, hungry for love. Always be aware of the importance love plays in every life. A person who feels the lack of love will often die inside; even if his body goes on living, the joy of living fades. Free sex is not the answer.

Barbara Cartland, world-renowned author of romance and true love stories, has sold more than 200 million books throughout the world. This proves people are still longing for pure clean love in their hearts.

You must have complete respect and admiration for another person before there can be true love. Without these, there can be no lasting love, so above all, never lose your own self-respect.

Youth has the most vital role to play in this, the most crucial period of mankind's unfolding. Technically, man has reached unparalleled heights. Teen-agers are the future of an even greater world. You can make tomorrow triumphant by what you think and do today.

BODY REFLEXES TO STIMULATE
SEX GLANDS FOR MEN AND WOMEN

Look at Diagram 2 and find the reflexes to the sex organs on the head and also the endocrine glands (pituitary, pineal, thyroid, parathyroid, thymus, pancreas, and adrenals). All these reflexes will stimulate the organs and glands named when pressed, massaged, or tapped. Light tapping with the fists or with the wire brush and also massaging with the fingers will bring renewed circulation.

First, we will turn to the reflexes in the pituitary glands, the thyroid, and the adrenals, which have a large influence on the gonads in both male and female. It has been scientifically proven that one of the main causes of disorder in the reproductive organs is an imbalance of hormones. By massaging the reflexes to these special endocrine glands, you are stimulating them to produce the hormones that are needed to normalize the gonads. See Diagram 5 of the hands and feet. Study the directions in the endocrine chapter for massaging the reflexes on the hands and the feet to open up channels that will send energy and a renewed flow of hormones into all areas of the gonads. This will bring them into healthy, normal harmony and balance with the whole system.

In Diagrams 10 and 11, notice the reflex buttons near the internal organs and glands. With the middle finger, or all the fingers grouped together, press into each one of these reflexes that are in relation to the sex glands, and also the reflexes that correspond with the endocrine glands. Press each reflex and count to three slowly, then release. Repeat until you have pressed each one five times. If there is a lot of fat involved, you will have to press in deeply to reach the reflex button. Do this gently so as not to bruise the flesh. Also press the reflex button to the solar plexus. See Photo 12 and press about one inch higher than shown for solar plexus reflex. Also, see Diagrams 10 and 15.

The Medulla Oblongata

Now, let us go to that vitality-generating reflex button, the medulla oblongata, which is called the power station of life forces. In Diagram 3 you will see the location of this all-important reflex button. When pressure is applied here, it prepares the body for sustained action; the impulses are funneled into it from your entire nerve network. It steps up vitality and relieves tensions, so you can easily understand why it is called a giant power station and will help in stimulating the sex glands.

With the middle finger of both hands, or just one finger, press this reflex button and hold to the count of three. Do this about five times to make sure all of the other glands are getting an equal flow of the life force.

MASSAGE OF THE ARMS AND LEGS

There are several reflex buttons that stimulate the sex glands on the arms and the legs, but rather than confuse you with too many reflexes to remember, I suggest that you use the reflex roller as illustrated in Photo 43. This will help you locate any hidden reflex buttons that may indicate blockages that you would not be aware of otherwise. Do not use this method on legs if you have varicose veins.

Roll the roller massager on the inside of the leg, starting at the ankle. Roll it up along the calf of the leg to the knee. You may want to roll this same area several times. Then, move the roller toward the front bone and roll up and down again. You will be amazed at the "ouch" spots you will find. It is no wonder that you have been having so many health problems! Remember, the blockage you are releasing here is not only going to the sex glands but to nearly every part of your body. Now, roll up and down on the outside of the leg. If you prefer to massage each tender button as you discover it with the roller, you may use the fingers to massage it out. I like to use the roller because it does work wonders in contacting a lot of blocked channels that would otherwise go untreated. It also stimulates the flow of the lymph fluid. Use the roller to search out any "ouch" buttons that might be in the calf of the leg. Don't neglect rolling it around the knees in various places. Be sure to do this to both legs.

Move to the upper legs, the thighs. Ah, here is where you will cry uncle! You will probably find so many very sore buttons that you won't believe it possible to have that many sore spots and not be aware of it. Starting at the knee on the inside of the leg, roll the reflex roller all the way up to the crotch. Continue rolling the whole leg. When you get to the outside of the leg, roll up onto the hip. You will probably find some "ouch" buttons here, also.

Remember, you do not have to press very hard to get results. In most cases, it does not take much pressure to loosen the obstructions and open the channels.

Now let us go to the arms and give them the same rolling reflexology treatment that you used on the legs. I like to use the same roller massager on other parts of the body too, as it seems to search out congested reflexes that I miss when using only my fingers and it does it in a much shorter time.

THE BACK

The back is also involved but it is impossible to massage the full length of the back by yourself, so let us hope you can find someone to roll the massager on each side of your spine. *Do not use the roller directly on the spine.* You can probably reach the lower part of each side of the spine by yourself with the roller massager. Do the best that you can if you have no one to help you. See Diagram 9B. Also massage the reflexes marked on the buttocks.

Another way to help stimulate the gonads is to massage the lower back muscles. Use the fingers here as you massage across the muscles from the spine to the hips with a rolling massaging motion.

USING REFLEX TONGUE PROBE

Another excellent way to stimulate the gonads is with the reflex tongue probe. This is a magic little massager that you can use to reach the reflexes to the gonads located on the tongue. See Photo 22. We have many stories of the wonderful results people are getting from using the tongue probe. Look at Diagram 16 on zone therapy and notice how the center lines run through the tongue and straight down through the gonads (uterus and penis). Now you understand why the reflexes in the tongue are sure to send the life force into the sex glands.

OVERCOMING IMPOTENCY IN MEN

For an added stimulation for those who feel they need still further help to overcome impotency, take the scrotum and its contents (testicles) in the hand and apply on and off pressure about twenty times (or more) a day. Let us look at a so-called "hot spot" which is located between the scrotum and the anus and another key stimulation button that is located between the tail-bone (coccyx) and the anus. Press and release these sex-stimulating reflex buttons with the fingers, gently, five times. Now, for further stimulation, press all around the anus. Massaging these sex-stimulating reflexes can be useful for women as well as men.

An Example from the Philippines

While I was in the Philippines, I met a lady who was going to a particular healer at the same time I was. She told me that her husband was impotent, but she was too embarrassed to ask if there was a way to help him. Since this healer and I were good friends and he was teaching me his ways of natural healing, I was not shy in broaching the subject to him. Using her as a patient, he showed me how to bring the blood to the area that would stimulate the sex organ. It was quite painful to her and she screamed and yelled, but he kept right on showing me what to do and telling her to listen and learn the technique.

He had her spread her legs while lying down and, placing his fingers on the inside of both legs near the rectum, he searched for the tender spots. He showed me how the vein crossed over the bony structure and was quite tender. Now, he kept pressure on this vein and pulled the blood up toward the clitoris (on men, the penis). He said the blood slows down in this protected area and all it needs is to be pulled up a few times to start the renewal of circulation, which will end all symptoms of impotency. He also pressed the blood down the inside of the leg to the heel.

This is easy to understand and also to practice. Because many of us have very little exercise in our modern-day living, it is easy to understand that the circulation of the blood is slowed down over the years. So, if you are having sex problems, this would probably be one of the main areas to work on.

YOUR VOICE AFFECTS YOUR MASCULINE VITALITY

I will give you a million-dollar secret from the Himalayan monastaries:

At a meeting, we learned that when a man's voice begins to become high-pitched, it is a sure sign that his masculine vitality is in a deplorable condition. The vortex at the base of the neck controls the vocal cords and is directly connected with the vortex below, in the sex center. What affects one affects the other. When a man's voice is high, his manly vitality is low.

You can increase the speed of vibration in these vortexes by lowering the voice. Listen to the deep voice of a virile man, and make yourself speak in a deep masculine voice as much as possible. Some of you may find this hard to do, but it will bring results. Your lowered voice will speed up the vortex in the sex center, which will improve your masculine energy.

A woman must be very careful not to let her voice become too low or it will cause her to act and think mannishly.

REFLEXOLOGY TO BUILD HEALTHY SEX ORGANS IN THE MALE

The most important glands to stimulate for healthy functioning of the gonads (sex glands) are the endocrine glands. Make sure that you massage the reflexes to these glands first, as explained in the chapter on endocrine glands. If any of these reflexes are tender, they may contribute to trouble with the sex glands. If you have ever suffered from a malfunction of the sex glands, you already know that it hurts from the waist down.

Let us look to the reflexes related to the penis and the testicles. There are many reflexes to these, but I have had such wonderful results with a few simple ones that I will not confuse you with many.

Press in on the sex reflex button about the width of the hand below the navel, either with the thumb or the fingers, and massage the area rather hard for a slow count of three. See Diagram 10.

On the inside of the leg, about one hand's width above the ankle (Diagrams 9C and F), is a reflex to the gonads. It will probably be very tender if you have any malfunctioning of the sex organs. Massage this reflex with the thumb, gently at first, until you work out some of the soreness. This might take several days. Do not massage too long at first, not over thirty seconds. The whole area may be sore, so take time and massage all the area near this "ouch" button. See Photo 55 and Diagrams 9C and F.

About three inches above the knee, on the soft area on the outside of the knee, is another very tender reflex. It will make itself known quickly if your sex glands are malfunctioning. See Diagram 9C. Use the same massage on this as you did lower on the leg.

Let us turn to a reflex on the back. You may have to have someone else help with this. If you try it yourself, place your hands on your hips with the fingers pointing toward the abdomen. Now, slide the hands toward the back. Just before you reach the spine, press in and find the tender reflex buttons. This will be in the vicinity of the lumbar disc. See Diagram 9B. Notice also the reflexes marked on the buttocks. Press these with one finger and hold for quick stimulation. These back reflex buttons are especially helpful to those who have problems with erection.

Now look below the ankles. Notice on Diagram 7 where the reflexes are located to stimulate the testicles and the penis.

Massage of the Heels

The next massage involves the heels. Yes, I mean the *whole heel*. You will not believe the pain that can be invoked by pressing the reflexes around the whole pad of the heel on both feet if you have any malfunctioning of the sex glands or colon or any part of the lower extremities. You will probably need one of the reflex devices, such as the hand probe or the comb, to get good results in this area. It may take several treatments to work out all of the tenderness. It is important that you do keep massaging the tender buttons until they are no longer sore, but not in one day.

Start with the fingers hooked under the pad of the heel near the center of the foot and press in with a massaging motion. See Photo 47. After a few seconds, move the fingers slowly around the heel pad. I am talking about the heel *pad*, not the bony part where the reflexes to the hemorrhoids are located. By looking at Diagram 8 you will see that the reflexes to the small intestines are also located near this area. So, if you want to rejuvenate your sex glands, you can see why you will have to clear up other problems of the lower area of the body.

Operation Avoided for a Baby

One of my reflexology students told me of her experience with her grandson. When the baby was born there was something wrong with his scrotum. The doctors said he needed to have an operation, but they would have to wait a few weeks to perform it, because he was too young to survive it.

Mrs. M.'s children did not believe in reflexology and made fun of her for practicing it. One night they asked her if she would keep the baby overnight, because they had to make a business trip and would rather not take the baby along with them.

After they were gone he cried a lot, so she took his little feet in her hands and started a general massage on the reflexes on the bottom of them.

When she touched one particular place, he would jerk his little foot as if it were hurting him. So every hour or so she went back and massaged the reflexes in his feet very carefully and gently for only a few seconds at a time. She did this several times while the baby was with her. The next morning when he took his bottle, he seemed to be taking milk normally and didn't cry anymore.

The mother and father picked the baby up and took him home. Nothing was said about his condition. Later in the day the daughter called her mother and said, "Mother, you didn't."

The mother said, "Yes, I did."

They both knew what they were talking about. She said, "I should tell you, my baby is well. The problem has completely vanished." And it was true. The baby was well and the operation was never performed.

Today he is a normal, happy, healthy three-year-old, and Mrs. M.'s daughter and son-in-law swear by reflexology. They feel it may have saved their baby's life.

Prostate Trouble Cured

Dear Mrs. Carter,

I am writing this letter to tell you how grateful I am for your wonderful work in reflexology. I am seventy years old but have suffered from prostate trouble for several years. I refused to be operated on and prayed for some kind of miracle. My sister handed me your book on hand reflexology and suggested that I try it. That book was the answer to my prayers. It was my miracle! I started getting relief almost immediately after massaging my wrists, and today I am completely well, thanks to you.

—Gerry J.

Dear Mildred Carter,

I want to tell you the great relief I have received by using the reflexology methods you described in your book. I am only twenty-two years old, but I have had prostate trouble for seven years. I felt that I was too young to have a prostate operation, so I suffered through it, going from doctor to doctor and drug to drug. None of them seemed to help.

I received your book and read how to press reflex buttons on the wrist for prostate trouble by following your directions. I was amazed at the sudden relief that I received by pressing on a certain area on my wrist, as described in the book. I couldn't believe what was happening. Suddenly, all pain was gone, just like that. I waited a few minutes. The pain didn't return, so I kept on massaging this area in my wrist.

Now, just two weeks since I started using reflexology, I can sincerely tell you that I have had no more problems with my prostate. It is wonderful. I never have to get up at nights, and my whole health has improved tremendously from giving myself complete reflexology treatments.

I feel like I should have been feeling all these years— energetic—and I have a new lease on life. I feel now that I can plan my life ahead to a successful future and find happiness, as I should have had all these years. I feel better now than I can ever remember feeling in all my life.

—D. L.

HOW TO HELP A STUBBORN CASE OF PROSTATE TROUBLE

Nearly all of the cases of prostate trouble that I have ever worked on with reflexology have been helped. Mrs. Therese Pfrimmer tells us how to go deeper than the reflexes and massage a seemingly hard band around the penis. If your massaging the reflexes to the penis does not bring you relief from prostate trouble after several days, you might try Mrs. Pfrimmer's method. See if there is a hard band around the base of the penis. If you find that this is so, try massaging this band with the fingers until it becomes pliable and eventually vanishes. Your physician should be able to tell you if there is any sign of a more serious problem before you go into this deep massage of the penis.

HOW TO BE A GREAT LOVER

Since sex is so important to health, I am going to give you men a few secrets to improve your health and bring a new complete happiness into your life.

There are a lot of men who would like to know the secret of successful love-making but have no idea where to turn for help. This knowledge is very important to the health and happiness of man and woman in marriage.

The secret is that the woman should be coaxed into orgasm. The reason so many women have trouble climaxing is because their partner "bangs" them. This *anesthetizes* the clitoris and numbs all feeling, and she becomes frigid. When the man teases his lover slowly and softly until her desire for him overpowers her, she will have an orgasm that will thoroughly satisfy her. Never rush the sexual experience. You should make love by being loving and doing gentle things to each other to excite each other.

Sexual pleasure can make us physically healthier and bring harmony and happiness into our lives.

HOW TO CONVERT SEX ENERGY INTO FINER FORCES

For those who are single and don't want sex without love, here is a special exercise to keep the sex urge subdued but alive.

First, relax completely for a few minutes; then sit up straight. Keeping the neck and head very relaxed, start breathing deeply. Take five or six breaths, close your eyes, and try to visualize a great force within you. Do not have any thoughts connected with sex at this time. Resume the deep breathing and, each time you inhale, imagine that you draw the sex energy upward from its center, the base of the spine. Each time you exhale, direct this force to the solar plexus or, if you prefer, to the brain, to be stored there. Keep on doing this exercise for a few minutes without interrupting the rhythm of your breath. If you are not used to doing these deep-breathing exercises, stop them if you begin to feel dizzy. You may resume them after three or four hours, if necessary. You must be able to will strongly that the sex energies rise upward before being directed to the solar plexus or the head. Thus, these energies are not wasted in the practice of self-gratification but are conserved by the system and are transmuted into a finer force, adding magnetism, vitality, and attraction to your personality. This exercise is beneficial for both men and women. You may do this exercise when you feel the sex urge, or you may do it at any convenient time.

Get a lot of exercise and do not use stimulating food in your diet. Be aware that caviar, fish, oysters, pork, celery, spiced pickles, and seasoned dishes are foods that excite the passions. Also, coffee, chocolate, and alcohol are stimulating to sexual desire.

An Exercise for Bladder Control

Here is a good exercise for women who have weak bladder control. It will strengthen the muscles of the lower extremities and also weak abdominal muscles.

When you sit on the toilet to urinate, squeeze the muscle shut to stop the flow of urine—hold—then release. Repeat as often as possible, at least ten times. When you pull the muscles together to stop the urine, also pull in on the muscles of the abdomen. You will be tightening and strengthening important body muscles pertaining to the gonads and a better sex life.

Mrs. K.'s Problem

Mrs. K. tells us of her experiences of not being able to hold her urine. She was a young mother and it got so bad she didn't dare leave the house. Her chiropractor told her to strengthen the muscles by doing the exercise described above. She did and has never had that problem since. She is now a grandmother.

A Wonderful Tonic

I cannot end this chapter without mentioning the wonderful help women of all ages get from the wonderful female tonic, "Lydia Pinkham"—a mixture of herbs. I gave it to my daughters as soon as they started to develop into womanhood and I still have a bottle of Lydia Pinkham on my shelf. I wouldn't think of being without it. I usually have to order it ahead, as it is becoming hard to get and some drugstores won't bother to order it. If I feel the least bit of stress in the area of my lower abdomen, I start taking the tonic—all symptoms of discomfort vanish within a day. You see, it relaxes the organs that tend to tighten up under stress. It accomplishes, on the inside, what reflexology does from the outside. The two methods correlate and help bring the miracle of harmony and relaxation back to the whole gonad system.

Reflexology Helps Girl Become Pregnant

I had a young girl come to me for treatment because she couldn't get pregnant. I treated her a few times and told her about the Lydia Pinkham tonic. In a very short time, she informed me that she was pregnant and she later gave birth to a perfect baby girl.

Lydia Pinkham is the best tonic I know of to carry one through the menopause. This may be of benefit to men also, when they reach the change-of-life age, in relaxing their gonads as it relaxes the female organs. I never knew when I went through the menopause; one month it was there and then it was gone forever, with no adverse effects. If you can no longer get Lydia Pinkham, then try your health-food store for special mixed herbs to take its place.

Using Reflex Tongue Probe

I want to tell you of the importance of the reflex tongue probe in helping relieve complaints of the gonads, especially in relieving cramps. You can see in Diagram 16 that line 1 runs down through the center of the body to the uterus. When you put pressure on the tongue by using the reflex tongue probe, you stimulate all areas along zone 1. See Photo 22. You will probably find some very tender reflexes here, especially near your period time. Many women carry a tongue probe in their purse at all times to help alleviate the pain of unexpected cramps and other symptoms of discomfort that might arise. Don't forget the value of the reflex comb. See the chapter on reflex devices.

This was used by medical doctors not too many years ago to alleviate all types of ailments, including headaches, earaches, backaches, and even to aid in painless childbirth.

HOW TO USE REFLEXOLOGY FOR PAINLESS CHILDBIRTH

This chapter would not be complete if I didn't tell you of a simple, natural method of painless childbirth. Reflexology is a boon to expectant mothers who choose to have their babies at home; they welcome this natural, painless method of delivery with no drugs or anesthetics to endanger their health and the lives of their unborn infants.

Do not use this technique before the baby is ready to be born. It might cause it to be born too soon and lessen its chances for survival.

The truly natural method of delivering a child is not to lie down but to stand on the feet and squat. This was the natural way native women had babies for hundreds of years. Some women still use their natural instincts to deliver in this method when they are not strapped down to a delivery table in a hospital.

With the help of two combs, a woman starting into delivery can press the teeth of the combs into the reflexes of her hands to help relax the muscles, allowing the baby to be born in a short time with very little pain. This makes the birth easier for the mother and the baby, reducing the likelihood of complications.

As soon as labor pains begin, the mother should be given a comb for each hand and something solid to press her feet against. Although ordinary household combs can be used, they are apt to break under pressure and injure the fingers. For this reason, reflex combs, which are specially designed for the purposes of hand reflexology, are recommended.

Holding the combs' teeth down, the patient exerts pressure across the tops by pressing down firmly with the fingers until the teeth dig into the palm area, as hard as can be comfortably borne and maintaining constant pressure. If the hands become tired, relax them for a few minutes; then continue the pressure. The combs should be held across the palm, or wherever it seems most comfortable to the patient. At the same time, press the soles of the feet hard against a footboard, which should have a rough rather than a smooth surface.

The patient might find more relief by turning the combs upside down and pressing the teeth into the tips of the fingers and the ends of the thumbs. See Photo 21.

Women in Labor Instinctively Use Reflexology Technique

This method of pressure on the hands has always been used by women in labor. It is a natural instinct to clench the hands or grasp the hands of anyone near. This is nature's own method of bringing relief from pain in labor. This is inadequate, however, because the pressure is not maintained for a sufficient length of time and because the means of the pressure is not sufficiently "sharp." Reflexology increases the effectiveness of an already existing method by improving on it.

Labor Pains Relieved by Reflexology

Reflexology relieves the nagging pains in the first stage of labor, not by retarding, but rather by promoting dilation. In the second stage, delivery is hastened and the mother delivers quickly and painlessly. Dr. White tells us that when using this method of helping the mother to a painless and quick delivery, there is absolutely no danger to either the mother or the child.

"Comb Lady" in Hospital

In Colorado, there is a woman known as the "comb lady," who works in and around the hospitals. Many women call on her for help at the time of delivery. She evidently knows just the right methods to use in helping expectant mothers to use the combs to have an easy and painless delivery. I hear many stories concerning this lady of mercy but have not had the pleasure of meeting her. She evidently uses the reflex comb to alleviate pain from other sources also.

You need no longer resort to harmful drugs to alleviate the pain and discomfort of being a woman. Turn to reflexology for all female problems.

And please teach your sons and daughters the true value of *love* in their lives and what it will mean in their future. Teach them how to keep the gonads (sex glands) in top performance by understanding and using reflex massage on all sex-related reflexes, thus guiding them into healthy and happy adults.

How Reflexology Saved an Unborn Baby

My daughter tried for several years to have a baby, with no success. When she did finally become pregnant, her doctor was not aware of it and operated on the uterus. She lost that baby at four months, and her doctor warned her she could never carry a baby, and if she did, it would have all kinds of defects. That really frightened her and her husband.

I told her that he was not telling the truth, so she changed doctors after she became pregnant again. When she was in her fourth month, the baby stopped moving! The stories the first doctor had told her came to mind, and she thought she would lose this baby, too. A friend's mother was a masseuse, so she went to her for help. The woman massaged and pressed on every reflex she knew, without results. Then she told her there was one last chance, and she pressed on a certain reflex button on top of my daughter's head. The baby gave a big kick and started moving around. They both cried with joy.

You can see that perfectly healthy baby girl in some of the pictures in this book.

Look at Diagram 2 for the reflexes on top of the head that go to the sex glands (gonads) and also those for the adrenal glands. The adrenal reflexes are probably what sparked renewed life and energy into the unborn baby. The body warmer reflexes, located along the top of the head, probably also helped by stimulating a weakening flame of life force. See Diagram 4.

An Old Maid Finds Love and Marriage

Dear Mrs. Carter,

I want to tell you of what has happened to me since I received your very kind letter about sex.

I told you how I had been raised by a puritanical mother who made sex something very dirty and sinful. This resulted in my being afraid of men and ending up an old maid. After receiving your letter and reading some of your suggested books, I have had a complete change of heart. I am quite attractive, even though I am in my early forties, and have no trouble finding boyfriends to take me out. It was very hard, at first, to be openly frank with men but I made it. To make a long story short, I am married to a wonderful man and so very happy. My big regret is that I did not meet you or have someone to tell me when I was a young girl that sex is love and is very beautiful when you are with someone you love.

—J. R.

Reflexology Awakens Frigid Wife after Forty Years

Dear Mrs. Carter,

I have been married for forty miserable years. I have a wonderful wife, whom I have always loved with all of my heart, but she was frigid all of those years. I thought she hated me! I got so I didn't bother to touch her or even kiss her anymore. Then, after talking to you on the phone, you sent your wonderful letter to both of us. It explained a lot of things about sex that neither of us knew about, making it sound like something beautiful and sacred in the name of love.

We had never discussed this subject openly before, but after reading your wonderful letter together, we decided to try your method. God, did it work. For the first time in our marriage, we feel like newlyweds. We are so grateful to you, and we hope you will help many others like us who have been living in the darkness of ignorance.

—M. B. & K. B.

19

How to Cure Hemorrhoids with Reflexology

The pain of hemorrhoids can be almost unbearable at times and also very embarrassing. Yet, with the simple technique of massaging certain reflex buttons, I have relieved hundreds of people permanently of this painful affliction. You can heal yourself by just pressing a few "ouch" buttons and feel the pain vanish like magic under your fingertips almost immediately. If you keep up the massage for several days, the hemorrhoids will disappear completely.

Hemorrhoids are varicose blood veins in or around the rectum. To find the reflexes to these troublesome and painful areas, first look to the feet.

USING FOOT REFLEXES

With the finger and the thumb, press on the bony part of the heel, just above the pad. You will find a ridge along this area. Press all the way around this ridge, searching for tender points. See Diagrams 7 and 8. You may have to use a reflex device to help you press hard enough to really massage the reflexes. The hand reflex massager seems to work well here. You will probably not find this whole area tender, just certain points. The swollen veins in the rectum causing the painful hemorrhoids are usually only in one or two places. You have to search out the "ouch" buttons and press and massage for several minutes. Sometimes these can be very painful, so start out with as much pressure as you can stand. Now, work your fingers slowly up under the inner ankle bone, pressing firmly, searching for "ouch" spots. Press and massage all along the back part of the leg with the fingers and the thumb on each side of the Achilles' tendon. You may find several tender reflex buttons in this area. Don't be afraid to massage them out no matter how painful it may be. Do this complete massage on both feet and legs. Also, check for a tender reflex behind the nails of the big toes.

USING HAND REFLEXES

We will turn to the reflexes in the hand to alleviate the pain of hemorrhoids. Press on the bony part of your wrist with the thumb of the opposite hand. Start on the palm side and press all of the areas on or below these bony areas; turn the hand over and press with the thumb or the fingers on the top of the wrist, still searching for the tender reflexes to the hemorrhoids. See Diagram 9A and Photo 40. Do this on both of the wrists. I have seen this technique completely heal some very bad hemorrhoid cases of long standing. There is also a reflex button on the end of the tailbone. Test this for tenderness also and massage it.

REFLEXES OF THE HEEL PAD

Another very important area of reflexes to the rectum area is located under the pads of the heels. If you have pain in any part of the rectum or lower colon area, you will find these reflexes so tender that you can hardly bear to massage them. Massage them you must, to relieve pain and get the flow of the electrical life force circulating into the problem area so as to help nature heal the inflamed, aching tissues. Remember, when any stimulation is applied to the surface of the body, a reaction will occur somewhere. This is a hard area to reach with the fingers, especially if the foot is callused, so you will probably have to resort to a device to help you reach these special reflexes.

You may first want to try your fingers as shown in Photo 47. Take the pad of the heel in the hand and try to press the tips of the fingers under the pad. If this does not get results, try the hand reflex massager or the reflex comb. Grasping the comb in both hands, roll it from side to side, giving special attention to the area that is located on the inside of the foot, up toward the ankle. This you may find extremely tender. Another way to massage these hard-to-reach reflexes is to use the rung of a chair or table. I discovered these important reflexes on the edge of my coffee table. Use whatever comes naturally until you get the soreness worked out. When the hurt stops in these reflexes, you will find that the hurt in the lower rectum area has also subsided.

Mrs. J.'s Story

Dear Mrs. Carter,

I have had a history of colon trouble for several years, as I told you earlier on the phone. I was visiting for several weeks and couldn't follow my diet. I began suffering terrible pain in the whole lower part of my body. I didn't want to bother anyone with my troubles, but I wasn't very jolly company. At night, the pain was terrible; I just lay there and suffered. Even aspirin didn't help. That is when I decided to call you, and you told me about the heel technique. Now I want to tell you what a godsend your advice was. That evening while everyone was watching television, I started massaging under the pad of my heel. I don't know when I ever had anything hurt that bad. Believe me, it took willpower to keep it up, but I knew I was really on to something when it hurt that bad! I only had my fingers to massage with, but I sat there all evening massaging under the heel pads. One foot was much sorer than the other, so I concentrated mostly on that foot. By the time we went to bed, a lot of the soreness was worked out, and would you believe that I slept all night without pain! I still do not have trouble in this area, and I cannot find any sore spots in the reflexes under my heel pads. I can't praise you enough for sending me the blessing of reflexology.

—R. J.

20

How to Use Reflexology to Relieve Asthma

Asthma is truly a dreadful disease, causing many frightening experiences for the sufferer. When you cannot breathe, your whole body is in trouble. Breath is life; many asthma sufferers die from lack of air in the lungs as well as side effects from the medication that is given for its relief.

An Asthmatic Recovers

A girl who worked for me suffered from asthma attacks that kept getting worse as time passed. Doctors were giving her medication that was very harmful to her body. Doctor J. told her that eventually the medication would kill her.

After a few costly stays in the hospital, she agreed to try reflexology. I sent her to one of my reflexology students who had become very proficient. After a very few treatments, she started to improve. At this date she is almost completely recovered. I also recommended that she take vitamins. They helped the body rebuild itself after the years of abuse it had suffered from the ravages of the asthma and the poisonous medications she had been taking.

USING BODY REFLEXES FOR ASTHMA

Now we turn to the reflexes in the body that can help stop an asthma attack. Four important positions will activate your electric lines, sending a surge of healing energy to the congested area causing the attack.

Look at Photo 56. Notice how the finger is pressed into the lower part of the neck. See in Diagrams 17A and C how the collar bones form a "V." Place the middle or index finger into this "V" and pull

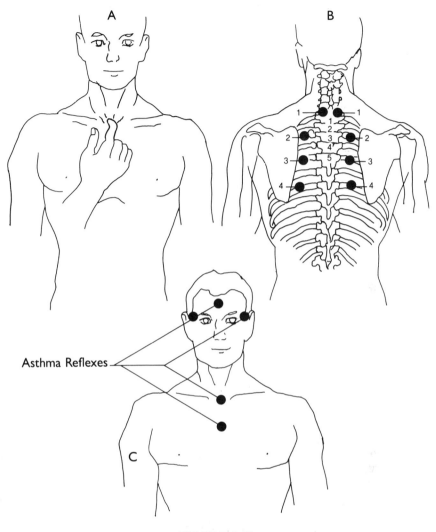

Asthma Reflexes

DIAGRAM 17

down while pressing firmly inward. Hold a few seconds, then massage downward. Do not press hard enough to bruise. This method is valuable in bringing quick relief from an attack of asthma.

There are reflex buttons on the spine that usually bring almost instant relief to an attack of asthma. It will be helpful if you have another person do the massage for you.

Study Diagram 17B. If you are alone, back up to the edge of a door frame and press the edge into the back as hard as you are able to. The spots will be very tender, but the attack will stop as if by magic as soon as you press on them.

If someone is there to help, either sit or lie face down on a couch or bed, or even on the floor, and have the person press on these spots with the thumb or finger. More than one finger may be used here if the added strength is needed, but it must be centered on the one spot. When another person is pressing on these reflex buttons, then opposites should be pressed at the same time.

When you find the correct buttons, which will be tender, press firmly and hold for a count of seven. I have seen this stop a bad attack of asthma instantly.

Now massage fairly hard toward the spine. Remember, these reflex buttons are not on the spine, but on the sides of the spine. Notice how #2 spreads lightly away from the spine and #3 spreads still farther toward the shoulder blades. If you have a reflex bar you may be able to use this successfully on yourself.

Immediate Relief from Asthma Attack

Dear Mrs. Carter,

I had been a sufferer from asthma for several years. I had taken all the tests for allergies, but the doctors could find nothing that I was allergic to, except cigarette smoke, so I avoided that. Nothing seemed to help. My husband wanted me to go to a reflexologist. After several more months of suffering and having to go to the hospital and be under oxygen, I decided to take his advice. I went to a professional reflexologist, who was one of your students.

She found certain spots in my body that relieved the coughing and gasping spells immediately. As soon as she touched certain reflexes on my back just below my shoulders and two inches below the neck simultaneously, the asthma attack subsided immediately.

She had decided that the adrenals were affected, and as she worked on the adrenal reflexes, the asthma attacks subsided.

Today, I have very few attacks. If I feel one coming on, I rush to my professional reflexologist to get immediate relief.

—J. M.

REFLEXES TO THE ADRENAL GLAND

The adrenal gland is the culprit that needs special attention when one is suffering from asthma.

In Diagram 5, see that the reflexes to the adrenal gland are located almost in the center of the hand and the foot. Massage these a few moments, and move to the top of the foot and the back of the hand. Press and search for a tender spot above the little finger and above the little toe toward the ankle.

Take the big toe between the thumb and forefinger and press. Search out a tender spot here, and hold or massage for a few moments. You may also do this to the thumb.

Asthma in a Child

I once had a child come to me suffering from asthma, which she claimed to have had since she was very young. No one knew what to do to relieve her.

I started in on her feet and worked on all of the reflexes that had any connection with asthma. I worked on all of the endocrine gland reflexes, which must always be done in any malfunction of the body, no matter what it is. See Diagram 5.

Remember, if just one of the endocrine glands is not functioning perfectly, this causes all of the endocrine glands to go out of tune and puts the whole body out of harmony.

I massaged all of the body reflexes that I have given you here so that we could stop the asthma and build up lasting protection against further attacks. I taught her how to massage these reflex buttons when she felt an attack coming on and told her to eat honey and to chew the honeycomb. In a short time she was completely free from all signs of asthma, and to this day she is a healthy happy woman with children of her own. She says she keeps her children healthy by using the miracle of reflex massage on them when needed.

AN ADDITIONAL HELP FOR ASTHMATICS

It has been learned by many doctors that when people have asthma the upper part of their lungs shows a lack of blood. Turning the patient upside down to allow blood to circulate into the upper part of the lungs relieves the patient considerably. Several helpful positions can bring the asthma sufferer relief. The most important is the yoga headstand. This may be difficult to do for many. There is a device now on the market that will enable anyone to stand on the head comfortably for a long period of time. It is called the "Body Lift." There are also slant boards available on the market that help reverse the pull of gravity on the entire body, increasing blood circulation to all parts of the body from the head to the feet.

Another way to get the blood circulating to the upper part of the lungs for quick relief is to lie across the bed on the stomach with the head resting on the hands or arms on the floor.

REFLEXOLOGY HELPS EMPHYSEMA

Use the same reflex buttons for emphysema as you used for asthma, concentrating on the endocrine gland reflexes.

There is a doctor who actually cured many patients of emphysema; some of them were already bed-ridden and in their seventies. He had them ride bicycles. He put stationary bicycles by their beds and had them start very slowly with just a few strokes at first. As their strength increased, he increased the time they were allowed on the bikes until they were able to ride real bikes outside. He tells us that some of these patients recovered enough to return to work. The motion of riding a bike seems to cause a different way of breathing that is beneficial to the area in which the emphysema is located.

Don't overlook the benefits of the "Rebounder." It is like a small trampoline that will fit in any room. This simple little exerciser makes it possible for us to use the three forces of nature—gravity, acceleration, and deceleration. Taking advantage of these forces, we can aid our bodies to overcome many ailments. It could even help a smoker to give up smoking.

MUSIC HELPS THE BREATH

I would like to interest you in music. You think this is not the place to talk about music? I think it is. There is a little instrument that you can hold in the palm of your hand, which makes beautiful music and can be played by anyone. And it will help build up your breathing power while you are having fun playing your favorite songs. It is the simple little harmonica. Surprised? Just try to blow one a few minutes to see how much wind it takes. If you practice making music or even just a pleasant noise for several minutes a day, you will find that your lungs become more powerful and you can play louder and longer. Start out with a small harmonica and work up to the double reeds later, since these take more wind power than the smaller single reed ones do. Don't get a cheap harmonica. They are not very expensive so start with the best. I prefer a "Marine Band." These come in several keys. It will be best to start with the key of C unless you are familiar with music. Books are available to teach you how to play many songs.

All of these devices will be beneficial to anyone with any type of lung weakness along with using the reflex massage on all of the reflex buttons I have described earlier.

If you really want to get back your breathing power so you can take a deep breath and feel the oxygen surging through your whole body, take the key I have given you, and open the door to a new life.

21

Treating Coughs and Colds with Body Reflexology

Colds and flu usually start with a sore throat, so let's cure the sore throat before it gets started enough to do real damage.

If I feel the slightest warning of sore throat, the first thing that I do is the lion posture from yoga. This simple posture stops a sore throat before it gets started. You may want to be alone because it certainly is not complimentary to one's looks, as you can see from Photo 57. Get down on your knees, sit back on your heels, place the hands on the knees, and spread the fingers apart as far as you can. Inhale a deep breath, and as you exhale the breath, stick out your tongue, straining to reach the chin with the tip of the tongue until you almost gag. Stiffen your fingers and bug your eyes out as you become very tense. Hold this position of tension for a few seconds, then relax. Repeat this posture four or five times, and you will be amazed to feel almost immediate relief from the sore throat. The lion posture rushes an extra supply of blood to the affected area. It tones and strengthens the muscles and ligaments in the throat.

A Yoga Posture Helps a Child

It is truly amazing how quickly this method stops a sore throat for all ages. I had my three-year-old granddaughter do this posture one day when she complained of her throat hurting. We made a game out of the posture and all got on the floor and did it with her. When she got up, she said, "I don't have an ow-ey in my neck anymore, Mommy." That was the end of the sore throat. My daughter was amazed even though she had been taught to use this posture since she was a young child. She said, "We get so involved with doctors and advertised drugs, we forget the true and simple healing methods of nature."

Healing in Strange Places

I have taught this posture to many of my friends, some in very odd places—like in the restroom of a large resort. A young woman with a bad sore throat was going to cut her vacation short and go home. She told me, "We planned this vacation for months, went to a lot of work finding the right person to stay with the children, got reservations almost a year ahead, and now, this! We really needed to get away by ourselves for a while. We have a whole two weeks and have only been here two days." She was crying and I cried too. I asked her if she would try an odd exercise to help cure the sore throat in a hurry. (I usually don't tell people that I am a reflexologist. They look at me so blankly, as if I am some kind of a freak.)

I had her put her sweater on the floor to kneel on and showed her how to do the lion posture. She did it several times, and when she got up, she looked at me in amazement. She felt her throat, swallowed a few times, and said it felt completely well. I showed her the reflexes on the feet and the hands, told her to massage any spots that showed tenderness, and advised her to do the lion posture whenever she felt she needed it. I also told her to get some apple cider vinegar if she could. If this was not possible, any kind of vinegar would do. She should dilute it with water and gargle often, swallowing a little each time she gargled.

I don't know when I have ever seen anyone so elated. She hugged me and cried with joy. She said that she would call home and tell her baby sitter what to do with the children if they developed sore throats. We saw her and her husband several times after that, and they were acting like happy newlyweds.

USING HAND REFLEXES

The reflex for the throat is located on the lower part of the thumb where it fastens onto the hand and all of that area including the web between the fingers. See Photo 37. This also holds true with the reflexes to the throat on the feet. Search for any tender spots anywhere on the big toe where it joins the foot. I have stopped many a sore throat by massaging this particular area. I find this so, especially, on very small children who cannot do the postures and people who are not able to kneel on the floor for the lion posture (Photo 57).

There is healing benefit in apple cider vinegar, especially in destroying germs. In Dr. D. C. Jarvis's book, *Folk Medicine*, he tells of the uses for and cures brought about by apple cider vinegar. One of them is its ability to cure strep throat.

An Unusual Remedy

I brought my eight-year-old granddaughter home to our ranch one summer. Her mother said the girl had been to a doctor for strep throat, but that she had been cured by medication. We were home about two days when I noticed that she was having a hard time swallowing. I looked in her throat and found it covered with white nodules. I knew the strep was back again. I immediately started giving her a mixture of two teaspoons of apple cider vinegar in a glass of water. I had her gargle this every half-hour and swallow a little each time. In a very short time, the throat was clear of all inflammation and the strep germs never returned.

EXPLORING THE TONGUE

Using the tongue probe is also very helpful in curing a sore throat. Just press the back of the tongue with the reflex tongue massager, feeling for tender buttons on the tongue. Some of these can be very sore, but remember what we say in reflexology: "If it hurts, rub it out." Since this is a sensitive reflex area for many malfunctions of the body, be sure to keep a check on any tender spots that might appear on the tongue. See Photo 22.

HELP FOR OTHER SYMPTOMS

Now that we have learned to eliminate one of the first signs of a cold, let us go to the other symptoms, such as sneezing and coughs.

When one has developed a bad cold, it is wise not to give complete reflexology treatments. A cold usually indicates that impurities have accumulated in the system, and that the body is trying to clean house by expelling these harmful toxic substances. When we massage certain reflexes, we are helping the body throw off poisons and taxing certain glands and organs, causing them to do extra work in helping the body clean house. So, the only reflexes we will work on during a cold are the pituitary reflex, which is located in the center of the big toe and the thumb, and the throat reflexes. Also, we can press and massage the reflexes to the lungs to help them utilize an added supply of oxygen.

You will see the special reflex buttons for the lungs as you study Diagrams 10 and 11. Press this whole area if you find tender spots on or near the reflex points. Also, search for tender reflexes in the ears and the body warmer buttons on the head. See Diagrams 4 and 15.

If you want to abort a cold before it gets started, take a coffee enema. I have done this many times, and it really works. Use about three teaspoons of instant coffee to a quart of warm water or make a pot of regular coffee and use it. It is said that it stimulates the liver. Do not use a coffee enema at night; it may keep you awake. Use honey instead.

Vinegar and honey is a good remedy to take orally, and don't forget the power of the onion and the magic healing properties of garlic. We all know that we must take a large amount of vitamin C to stop a cold or to help get over one quickly. Take a lot of lemons, but not oranges or grapefruit. Massage the pituitary reflexes to lower a fever.

How a Bad Cough Was Stopped Instantly

While I was in a large hotel in Hawaii, I noticed that one of the maids had a very bad cough. She hardly stopped coughing between breaths. When we went out into the hall, I walked up to her and said, "Here, hold your finger like this." I showed her how to squeeze the joint near the end of her middle finger with the fingers of the opposite hand. She looked very puzzled and doubtful until an older Hawaiian maid came and said, "You do what she says, she knows." So the girl did as I told her and she stopped coughing almost immediately.

When we came back several hours later, she greeted me with the greatest enthusiasm—she couldn't thank me enough. There was no sign of the cough that had been troubling her earlier. We were there for several days, and I never heard her cough again.

I hope that you will pass the sensational principle of simple reflex massage onto everyone that might meet with a hard-to-overcome health problem. And then tell them to pass the information on to others. In this way, you will light one more candle to send out healing light to a sick and suffering world.

Reflexology for Bronchitis

Dear Mrs. Carter,

I know that everything you say in your books is true. I use so many of your methods to help friends and loved ones and myself. I will tell you of one experience I had.

One morning, I got up with a very bad cough. I was gagging and was very sick, so I went to a doctor. After looking at my throat and X-raying my chest, he said I had bronchitis. I informed my father-in-law of my problem and he used reflexology treatments on me as described in your book. I went back to the doctor in a few days and he said that I was well. Now, when I get sick, I go to my father-in-law and he makes me well. Everyone, young and old, should have your reflexology books in their home library. Thank you.

—Mrs. M. N.

22

How Reflexology Can Cure a Headache

Headaches have many different causes—tense nerves, stress, eye strain, upset digestive system, and hangovers, besides malfunctioning organs or glands in the body. Millions of people turn to drugs to get temporary relief. Now, you can turn to nature and reflexology and learn sure, quick ways to stop a headache almost immediately. You can do it yourself anyplace the headache strikes—home, office, at a party, while camping, etc. Because reflexology tends to heal the whole body by opening up closed electrical lines, it prevents the headache from recurring.

Look at Diagrams 2, 3, and 4. No wonder the head can ache in so many places. Notice all of the reflex buttons on the head and face. When you think that each one of these is connected to an electrical channel that leads to some part of your body, you can readily understand why the head can ache.

USING HAND REFLEXES

Let us start with the reflexes in the hands. These are the simplest, easiest reflexes to reach in any emergency. Since the reflexes in the thumbs represent the head area, first massage the thumb reflexes. With the thumb of the opposite hand, start pressing on the center of the pad of the thumb; then squeeze the sides of the thumb by pressing each side of the nail. With a firm pressure, massage just below the thumbnail on top of the thumb, searching for tender buttons. See Photo 58. Cover the complete thumb with the searching massage; remember, do not rub the skin, but the reflexes under the skin. If you don't find a sore spot on one thumb, change hands and give the other thumb the same massage. When you do find an "ouch" spot, massage it for several minutes or until the head stops aching. This usually works nine times out of ten.

If the headache persists, place the thumb on the web of the opposite hand between the thumb and forefinger. Pinch and massage this whole area, clear up to where you feel the bones come together, searching for tender buttons. See Diagrams 9A and D and Photo 37. This reflex stimulates many parts of the body, so if you find an "ouch" spot here, be sure to rub it out. If you can't find a sore spot here, change hands and do the same to the opposite hand. Since this is one of the crucial reflex buttons for the whole body, it is a good idea to keep this area free from sore spots at all times.

If the headache *still* persists, press and massage the reflexes in the center of both hands, searching for tender buttons. The magic massager will be useful here—it should be used every day to help keep these reflexes stimulated and the electrical life lines open to every part of the body.

USING FOOT REFLEXES

You will find that massaging the reflexes of the feet works miracles, not only for headache but for any other health problem that you might have. Massage all the reflexes, starting with the big toe and going over it, just as you did on the thumbs and the hands. See Diagram 9E. Massage all the reflexes in each foot, searching for tender reflex buttons. You may find the reflexes in the feet to be more sensitive than anywhere else on the body. I believe these reflexes in the feet to be most powerful of all in their ability to stimulate the healing life force to every part of your body by opening up closed or clogged electrical lines.

This is why I so highly recommend the reflex foot massager. It is easy to use while you are watching television, talking on the phone, or sitting anywhere. See Photos 44 and 45. It will really stimulate the *healing universal life force* within every part of your body and touch the malfunctioning area that is causing the painful headache. If you haven't already overcome the headache, let us go on to other reflex buttons.

MASSAGING THE HEAD

Look at Diagram 3; see the button called the medulla oblongata at the base of the skull. This button is important in addressing several health complaints that are mainly caused by stress. This is what we call a stress button. Pressing it will bring relief to several health complaints besides a headache. Since its location makes it hard to find and control the pressure needed, you will find it more convenient to use the hand reflex massager. You do not need to press very hard on this particular reflex, just firmly enough to feel the pressure in your head.

Look at Photos 4, 6, 7, 8, and 54 to see how the fingers are being pressed on many areas of the head at once. Use a light but firm pressure as you move the fingers onto different reflexes with a slightly rotating massage. Remember, you are massaging reflexes under the skin, not the skin itself. If you find any reflexes painful to the touch, massage them for a few minutes. Massage the reflexes around the ears and also search the ears for tender reflexes. Keep massaging on down the side of the neck to the shoulders and along the top of the shoulders. See Photo 41. Massage all of the muscles in the back of the neck to relieve tension that may be slowing the circulation to the brain, eyes, and other organs within the head. See Photo 5.

DEALING WITH FREQUENT HEADACHES

If your headaches are frequent, look for added relief by massaging all the reflexes in the body as shown in Diagrams 10 and 11, using the same method you learned in the chapter on massaging the body reflexes.

Don't forget to do relaxing meditation every day.

Many a headache is caused by the spine being out of place, so if the headache still persists after these treatments, be sure to check this out with your chiropractor.

OTHER METHODS FOR HEADACHES

You may need to change your diet by eating lots of fresh vegetables and fruits, avoiding sugar and chocolate and (for some people) coffee and dairy products. *Don't overeat.* This is the most common sin against health committed by the American people. We eat too much. I can remember people saying that my grandparents didn't eat enough to keep a bird alive. They lived healthy lives to the ages of 99 and 103.

Edgar Cayce told many of his people to sit with the back straight and bring the chin forward to touch the chest, then tilt the head back as far as possible to help open the flow of blood in the pipelines leading to and from the head. I knew a woman who did this 100 times every day and she threw away her glasses. Don't do this more than five times at first, or you will develop a headache from tight and sore muscles.

One of the best ways to relieve a headache is to do a lot of walking, especially if you do it in the fresh air. Be sure to wear good shoes.

I have given you many ways to banish your headache forever. You will not need to do all these techniques—choose the ones that seem to help you the most, and live the rest of your life in health, free from pain.

HOW TO CURE A MIGRAINE HEADACHE

If you feel that you have what is called a migraine headache, the first thing to do is look for the cause. Many people have suffered for years from terrible headaches, only to discover they were caused by an allergy to a simple household item. Some migraines are caused by the spine or the neck being out of adjustment. Many headaches are caused by additives in food or by air pollution.

I know of many people who have rid themselves of what they called migraine headaches by using the simple method of reflex massage. After you have pressed the reflex buttons on your body, including the reflexes on the hands and feet, search the neck and head for tender buttons that will give you a clue to the cause of your pain. Work on all the reflexes involved. Keep the thymus active by tapping it often, and smile a lot. See Photo 9.

My daughter had terrible headaches for years; the muscles on the back of her neck would tighten up, stopping the circulation of blood to her head. She moved out of the valley into the mountains and her headaches stopped almost completely. When she went to town in the valley, she always came home with a terrible headache. Reflex massage helped, but we couldn't get at the cause until we discovered that the culprit was the smog. It had been causing what we thought were migraine headaches.

You should be able to find the cause and eliminate your headache by testing your reflex buttons and massaging all tenderness out. If the cause is an allergy or additives in your food, then you must eliminate this cause by experimenting.

Especially massage the medulla oblongata at the back of the head. See Diagram 3. Also massage the reflex buttons halfway between the medulla and the ears. See Photo 5. Massage the pain reflexes, the web between the thumb and forefinger, and also between the large toe and the second toe. See Diagrams 9A, D, and E. Massage the reflexes to the stomach on the hands, feet, and body. See Diagrams 6, 8, 10, and 11.

FAINTING OR DIZZY SPELLS

To overcome fainting, you must immediately get your head lower than your heart. When I was pregnant and felt a dizzy spell coming on, I would pretend to fix my shoe and no one noticed that I was stopping a fainting spell. After you get the blood to your head, press hard between your nose and lip. See Photo 49. Press the adrenal reflex button in the center of each hand and also the center of each foot. See Diagram 5. Press your fingernails into the center pad of the thumbs, reflexing the pituitary and pineal glands.

When you have time, check all of your reflexes to find the cause of your dizzy spells, and massage them out.

To stop a seizure, grab the thumb and pull it back hard toward the wrist. See Photo 59.

Son Helps Teacher at School

Dear Mrs. Carter:

I want to tell you what my son David, age 11, did for his teacher while in school.

David's teacher gave the class an assignment and asked them if they would study quietly as he had a terrible headache. David walked quietly up to Mr. J.'s desk and started to gently use pressure on certain reflexes on his head.

We didn't even know he knew how to do this. He had fun watching you when you came to the house and cured his father's headache about a month ago.

Mr. J., his teacher, came to see us that very evening wanting to know what David had done and where he had learned it.

In his words he told us, "I was in so much pain I could hardly stand it. I had taken aspirin with no relief, and suddenly I was aware of a soft touch on my head. I thought for a moment it was an angel touching me. Maybe, I thought, I had died." He laughed. "It seemed my head quit hurting almost instantly. I opened my eyes and there stood David doing all these weird pressures on my head with his fingers. Not only was my headache gone, but I felt physically great. Usually after one of these bouts I feel drained and ill for several hours. David said it was reflexology. I had to come over and learn more about it. I have never had such complete relief in my life."

He thinks David is a natural healer. How can we ever thank you for showing us all these simple natural methods of healing?

—Mrs. J. S.

23

How to Use Special Reflexology Devices to Relieve Pain

Dr. Fitzgerald made use of several devices found in the kitchen to help him hold a steady pressure on the reflex buttons for a long period of time. In cases of toothache, earache, labor pains, painful back, and many other painful ailments, he found he could deaden the part of the body to which the reflex went. To save time and to enable his patients to treat themselves at home, Dr. Fitzgerald showed them how to use such common devices as rubber bands, rubber balls, clothespins, and combs.

Reflexology is a natural way to health, and it is not essential that you have reflex devices to obtain benefits. The natural use of your fingers will work wonders in releasing the universal flow of the vital force and sending it surging through all the channels of your body. However, rubber bands, a comb, or another such device can be helpful in putting steady pressure on reflex buttons.

During my years of giving reflexology treatments, I devised several improvements over such old-fashioned implements. You can see my reflexology devices in use in several of the illustrations. You can use these devices safely in your home, your office, or while travelling. If for some reason you cannot find the reflex devices I describe below in your local health food or drug store, they are available at Stirling Enterprises, Inc., Box 216, Cottage Grove, Oregon 97424.

You will often need assistance in reaching many of the reflexes, both for massaging and for holding a steady pressure on many locations. My reflex massagers enable you to get this help.

REFLEX FOOT MASSAGER

Look at the reflex foot massager. It is simple to use, yet packs a healing power that you will never want to be without. Just place the massager on the floor; using it on a rug will keep it from slipping. Place both of your feet on the ridges of the massager and roll them back and forth. You will find you can massage most of the reflexes in your feet this way. After some practice, you will be able to use these ridges to massage along the reflexes to the spine, the eyes, and so on. There are raised buttons in the center of the reflex massager which will help reach into certain deeper, hard-to-reach reflexes in the feet. See Photos 44 and 45.

If you spend time in front of the TV, this reflex foot massager is invaluable. Just sit back and relax, place your feet on this magic reflex roller, and massage away all of your aches and pains. *Don't use for very long at first*. You will probably find yourself more relaxed than you have felt in years. Many people report that they never knew what a good night's sleep was until they started using reflexology. Remember, you are helping nature rejuvenate the entire body—naturally.

The Purpose of the Pressure

The purpose in using reflex pressure is to release local contraction of muscles and blood vessels or constriction of other soft tissues. Reflexology breaks a vicious cycle occurring in local short-circuited nerves. A reflexology treatment improves lymphatic drainage and steps up your blood supply. It releases waste products that have collected in local areas in amounts sufficient to cause discomfort and pain.

REFLEX ROLLER MASSAGER

Let us now look at the reflex roller massager. This is being used throughout the world by many grateful people. This beautiful little roller will search out every tender reflex button in your body. You can use it to roll over the bottoms of your feet and on your ankles, for your gonads. You can run the little roller up your leg close to the calf, move it over, and run it up the leg closer to the bone to the knee, and under and around the knee, all the time searching for tender reflex spots. It will be hard for you to realize that you could have so many tender spots in your body. Use this reflex roller on the outside of your leg also, up the thigh on the outside, rolling it in many places on the leg, holding a light pressure. When you come to a tender button, run the roller back and forth over the button or, having found the spot that needs to be stimulated with the universal life force, press and massage it with your fingers for a few seconds.

You may use this little magic roller anywhere on your body. It is great to have a partner massage the back, up and down each side of the spine. Do not massage directly on the spine with the roller or any device that you might have. A light pressure on certain vertebrae where directed is okay.

Look at the illustrations of the various uses of this reflex roller. See Photos 14, 15, 31, 33, 36, 43, 46, and 60. Remember, you heal the whole body by opening up closed electrical lines to allow the universal life force to flow freely. You will be amazed at the phenomenal results that you will get from using this roller massager to help you find all the buttons leading to blockage of the energy field.

REFLEX HAND PROBE

Now, let us look at the fantastic little reflex hand probe that is being used throughout the world. It takes the place of your fingers and keeps them from becoming tired. Many people's hands are too weak to press the reflex buttons properly. Their fingers get tired, so they turn to this handy little reflex hand probe. It can be used on any reflex in the body where your fingers would otherwise massage. See Photos 30, 35, 37, and 61 showing this fantastic little hand probe being used.

Many people tell me that they have used a pencil, but a pencil is hard to hold and the eraser usually breaks off, so they turn to the reflex hand probe to simplify their reflex treatments. It helps them heal the whole body by opening up closed electrical lines for full circulation of the universal life force to all glands, organs, and cells. This will help you retain complete health throughout your long life.

MAGIC REFLEX MASSAGER

An improvement on a rubber ball, the magic reflex massager presses reflex buttons in the hand when squeezed. See Photo 51. Since developing this device, I have received hundreds of letters from all over the world telling me of the unbelievable results people are getting. They are using this massager to press the reflexes in their hands and stimulate every part of their bodies.

When you begin to use this little magic massager, start out slowly—do not press with it for over two minutes at a time. It is so powerful in the way it stimulates the reflexes to so many glands at once, that to release all this new life force suddenly is a shock. The glands are shocked after they have been almost dormant for a long period of time.

How to Use the Magic Reflex Massager

Take the magic massager in one hand and squeeze your fingers around it. This will make its own little "fingers" press into several reflexes of your hand at once. Roll it over and the massager will press into a different set of reflexes. Each time you roll it a little, it reaches different reflex points. See Photos 34 and 62.

Roll it in your hand for about two minutes, then change the massager to your other hand, again massaging for about two minutes. You will immediately feel a stimulation of magnetic vitality surging throughout your entire body. You will not want to lay this little magic reflex massager down, but *remember—do not overmassage!* You can pick it up and use it again the next day, or maybe later in the same day. Every individual is different. If your body is in poor condition, use your magic reflex massager for short periods of time at first, with longer periods between massages. Do not try to make yourself completely well in one day.

You can also use the magic reflex massager in both hands at once. Place it in the palm of your left hand. Now cup your right hand over the massager, clasping your fingers around each other. Start rolling your massager in several directions. Feel how the little knobs press into the reflexes of both hands simultaneously. Use this same rolling-pressing motion on your thumbs and on each of your fingers.

The magic reflex massager is helpful in many sports activities. Golfers find that this device provides just the right amount of strength to the muscles needed to swing the club properly. Bowlers find the massager very helpful in keeping their hands and arms strong and relaxed.

Some people use two magic reflex massagers at once, one in each hand, for double benefits. If you look at Diagram 16, you can see how, with two massagers, you can stimulate the reflexes to most of the organs and glands on both sides of your body. By pressing massagers firmly with both hands, you will feel tension on every muscle in your body, especially in the inner muscles around your glands and organs.

Reflex exercises for the lower part of your body will not only benefit the lower lumbar area, but also the bladder and urethral channel. They will benefit the reproductive organs to such an extent that many persons feel a renewed interest in sex, as if they have been rejuvenated.

Warning: Don't overdo this the first week, or you will become very sore and think something has gone wrong with your organs.

Exercise only once a day for the first two days, then increase to two times a day for two days, etc., until the muscles have adjusted. This is the same as if you overexercised your legs or arms and got cramps in the muscles. Don't get cramps in the inside muscles. Just take it easy the first week or two, and you will find yourself becoming a new and beautiful you, thanks to the miracles of nature and reflexology.

TONGUE CLEANER

For centuries, long before modern mouthwashes came into existence, people in the Orient relied on a natural method for clean, fresh breath—tongue cleaning. You too can use a tongue cleaner to remove odor-causing film deposits. *The tongue cleaner cleans what the toothbrush does not!* In fact, your toothbrush was never intended or designed for your tongue. Use a tongue cleaner after you brush your teeth. Your toothbrush and your tongue cleaner are a perfect combination for superior and complete oral hygiene.

Before you use a tongue cleaner, sterilize it in boiling water for five minutes, or put it in an automatic dishwasher.

Hold the cleaner at both ends, with the middle, curved portion pointing into your mouth. Stretch out your tongue and slowly and gently scrape the upper surface of your tongue with an inside-out motion. See Photo 23. Hold the cleaner under running water to wash off the sticky deposit. Now, you can understand how unclean your tongue was. Repeat the scraping procedure as many times as you feel it is necessary, usually four or five times. Once you get used to cleaning with the tongue cleaner, adjust the scraping pressure to your needs.

At regular intervals, sterilize your tongue cleaner. It is not good hygiene to have more than one person use the same tongue cleaner.

If you are using the tongue cleaner for the first time, your tongue may feel sensitive for a week or so. If this happens, do not be alarmed, no harmful results will occur. Children may use the tongue cleaner but they should be supervised by an adult.

PALM MASSAGER

The palm massager is a small rubber ball that is still used by many doctors to strengthen the muscles in the arms. It is used in many hospitals to help arthritis sufferers and those overcoming paralysis from various causes.

REFLEX COMB

Pressing and massaging the reflexes with the fingers will give satisfactory results most of the time, but in certain cases a steady pressure will be needed for several minutes at a time. For this, use a comb. You can use any type of comb in an emergency, but keep in mind that most combs are made of plastic. You could very easily break and injure the hands or fingers if too much pressure is placed on the teeth. Therefore, in reflexology, doctors recommend that a metal comb be used. The vibrations of the metal are also thought to help in stimulation of the life forces. Certain metals give off "rays" or "vibrations" that stimulate the current of life forces in the body.

The metal comb is very helpful, for it reaches several reflexes at one time. In Photo 21, you see the tips of the fingers being pressed onto the teeth of the comb while the thumb is pressing on the end of the comb. The teeth of the comb can be used in the webs between the fingers. Also, you can use the back of the comb for a firm, steady pressure.

Other Uses for a Reflex Comb

Take the comb in your hand and press the teeth into the tips of your fingers, pressing your thumb on the end of the comb as shown in Photo 21. If you have two combs, use them both, one in each hand, for a vitalizing sensation of renewed life force.

Try putting the teeth of the comb in different positions. Press the teeth into your first finger on all sides, at the same time pressing your thumb on the end of the comb. This stimulates two important endocrine glands, the pituitary and the pineal. You should feel renewed exhilaration almost instantly. Use this method on all your fingers.

You may also apply the reflex comb effectively on the feet. Press the comb along the pad of your heel to reach all your foot reflexes in this area, working the teeth of the comb down toward your instep, keeping the teeth pressing under your heel pad. Hold pressure on all sore reflexes for a slow count of seven, then release and press again. Repeat this three to five times.

REFLEX CLAMPS

Spring clothespins and rubber bands have been used to press down on reflexes. Reflex clamps, now available, are safer, more comfortable, and easier to use. Many doctors have employed these simple devices to anesthetize various parts of the body and to cure many ailments.

Reflex clamps on the fingers help to relieve pain quickly, and in many cases permanently. Dr. Bowers states, "This pressure therapy has an advantage over any other method of pain relief, inasmuch as it has been proven that, in contradistinction to opiates, when zone [reflex] pressure relieves pain, it likewise tends to remove the cause of the pain."

In Photo 63 we see that the clamps are on the third, fourth, and fifth fingers of the right hand, stimulating the outer edge of the head and glands and organs on the right side of the body. If the left hand's thumb and second and third fingers are clamped (see Photo 52), we are treating the central part of the left side of the head and corresponding body organs.

Reflex clamps keep a steady pressure on the reflex buttons, so you can control several different reflexes at once instead of just one reflex point at a time. This lets you control pain and illnesses faster and more conveniently, especially if you are too ill or in too much pain to press each reflex button with your fingers for any length of time. These clamps may be used on one or several fingers at a time, on your earlobes, or on the webs between the fingers. See Photos 18 and 38. They can also be used on the toes.

Using Reflex Clamps for Vitality

Dear Mrs. Carter,

I cannot tell you how pleased I was at my first use of your reflex clamps. When I put them on my toes they seemed to stimulate my internal organs and cause my general vigor and vitality to improve by at least 100 percent.

—L. C.

TONGUE DEPRESSOR OR PROBE

A simple tongue depressor solves many health problems. By pressing the reflexes on the tongue, you can stop headaches, toothaches, abdominal pains, menstrual cramps, sore throat, and many other complaints. See Photo 22. It is convenient to carry in your purse and billfold so it can be used in sudden emergencies. *Warning! If you are pregnant, do not use the tongue depressor;* it relaxes the reproductive organs and might cause a miscarriage.

WIRE BRUSH STIMULATES REFLEXES

A wire brush is in several photos in this book.

When you tap the reflexes gently with the metal wires of the brush, you stimulate your electrical life force into immediate action in the area being contacted. The brush is not only great to brush your hair with, but also, when you use it as directed to tap your head and other areas of your body, it can stimulate your whole being into renewed energy and vitality. See Photo 3.

THE MIRACLE OF THE MINIATURE TRAMPOLINE

Bouncing on a miniature trampoline stresses every cell in your body, over and over again, approximately one hundrd times a minute. Every cell is strengthened by this stress. This constant pull and release on all of your body cells at the same time helps them become firm and strong.

Henry Savage, M.D., says, "Never in my thirty-five years as a practicing physician have I found any exercise method, at any price, that will do more for the physical body than the rebound exercise."

I know of no more powerful way to build your body into perfect health and keep it that way than by stimulating healthy cell growth with a combination of reflexology and exercising on the rebounder trampoline.

BED RAISERS

Many people raise the foot ends of their beds so they sleep with their heads downward. Thus, for awhile, they reverse the downward pull of gravity on their bodies. The constant daytime downward pull on our bodies is a cause of aging. Body cells become weak and the body tissues begin to sag downward. Even our bones begin to shrink from the constant downward pull of gravity. Thus you need to get your head lower than your heart at least part of the time. Bed lifters, which you place under the foot of your bed, reverse the downward pull of gravity while you sleep. You may lift the foot of your bed either three or six inches with these gravity-reversing bed lifters to reverse the process of aging.

24

Reflexology's Sensational Way to Beauty

THE IMPORTANCE OF BEING BEAUTIFUL

We all want to be beautiful from the time we are small children until we become centenarians. *You are beautiful!* Maybe you don't think you are, but you are truly beautiful and I am going to show you how to bring your true beauty out into the open where it shows.

Perfect health is the first requirement for beauty. To be beautiful, we must radiate health. I will give you a new way to capture vibrant health and beauty you never dreamed was possible for you, if you will only follow my directions. To be radiantly beautiful, you will have to be radiantly healthy and beautiful on the inside—keeping beautiful thoughts at all times. You already know how to use reflex massage to turn a tired, sick body into one vibrant with energy and health. Now, let us turn to reflex massage to give you a perfect petal-smooth skin and to keep it beautiful the rest of your life.

Of first importance is to have the endocrine glands in good condition. Keep them healthy by massaging the reflexes to these glands. See Diagram 5.

AN AID TO SKIN BEAUTY

Because I have always had a very sensitive skin and all soaps and cosmetics caused a rash, I searched for many years to find the perfect lotion to bring out the beauty of my skin and keep it beautiful. In my search for a healing, moisturizing skin lotion that contained only pure natural ingredients, I discovered *aloe vera,* the miracle plant. Ancient aloe vera juice has incredible benefits. I combined it with modern vitamin E and other rich emollients to banish such common skin problems as wrinkles, blemishes, age lines, dry flaky skin, brown spots, crepey throat, and acne and to help the skin retain moisture.

Aloe vera is a genus of plant belonging to the lily family. It is a succulent plant, originally from North Africa, used throughout the world as nature's miracle healing plant. For more than 3000 years, aloe vera reportedly has been used for medicinal purposes. One of the earliest written references to this plant is in the Bible, John 19:39. In biblical times aloes were very valuable. It is said that the women of ancient Egypt and Greece used the gel from the aloe vera plant to improve their complexions and skin textures. It is believed that Cleopatra's beauty can be credited to this plant.

Mildred Carter's Aloe Vera-E Cosmetics are available to you through Stirling Enterprises, Inc., Box 216, Cottage Grove, Oregon 97424.

A DO-IT-YOURSELF FACE LIFT AT HOME

Everyone hates to look in the mirror and see the lines of age start creeping into his or her face. More and more people are turning to cosmetic surgery to have these lines removed—if they can afford the price. Millions of dollars are spent on advertised skin remedies for trying to cover up these telltale signs of age. In previous chapters, I have told you how to massage certain reflexes to overcome every type of ailment. Now, I am going to tell you how you can use reflexology to give yourself a face lift and keep that youthful look the rest of your life.

A very successful studio in the East gives face lifts by redirecting and controlling the muscles in your face and neck with massage. The cost is just as high as the surgical face lifts.

With this revolutionary method, I will show how you can actually use reflexology to give yourself an *at-home* face lift by pressing certain reflex buttons on your face with your fingers. If you will take the time and follow directions closely, you will be able to erase a decade of wrinkles, creases, and crow's feet.

There are several doctors who praise this method. Dr. Willner, author of the book, *Touching Is . . .* , says that the earlier you get at the wrinkles, the better off you are. This treatment works especially well for middle-aged women and men.

With reflexology, you have a safe, simple, effective means of achieving a face lift without the risks of surgery—no painful post-operative period and no doctor's fees.

Look at Photo 64 and notice how the various dots covering the face are numbered. When you use this technique of reflex massage, excessive muscle tone is relaxed and sagging muscle tone is tightened. Dr. Maurice Gunsberger of Syosset, New York, has used this method with great success. He tells us, "You can really see a difference in the people who use this technique. It can make you look ten to fifteen years younger."

Many experts agree that you can reduce wrinkles and improve your looks with this technique of face reflexology, but they also agree that dry skin is a major cause of the skin wrinkling. While doing this method of face reflexology, it is of the greatest importance to use moisturizing creams to achieve the best results. This is where my Aloe Vera-E lotions will help keep your skin soft and moist twenty-four hours a day.

This technique is a bit complicated and you will have to follow directions very carefully if you *really* want a do-it-yourself face lift at home.

You will have to follow the pressing or tapping of these certain buttons on your face for a specified time. For the first five weeks, do this special massage three times a week. For the next three weeks, do the exercise two times a week. Then, once a week for the next two weeks. After this, put yourself on a maintenance schedule of once every two weeks.

Relaxing the Reflex Buttons

Sit in a comfortable chair. Have a watch with a second hand ready to time yourself.

See on Photo 64 that the reflex buttons are clearly numbered for each wrinkle group. Most buttons will be on both sides of your face, so use both hands as you treat both sides of your face at the same time.

This method of rebuilding sagging face muscles is different from massaging the reflexes in the face for stimulating certain glands and organs in the body. For this treatment, we will use the pads on the fingertips. This will involve *relaxing* each of the buttons listed. With the tip of the middle finger, press firmly and deeply enough to create mild discomfort; hold for ten seconds. Gradually release the pressure for ten seconds. Repeat about five times, using your watch for timing.

The next step is to *tonify* the buttons listed. Tap the areas lightly with the fingertips, with brief pauses every ten seconds.

If you do all the exercises, it will take approximately an hour. Can you afford an hour three times a week to regain a beautiful, firm, youthful complexion?

You do not have to do the whole face lift procedure. Maybe you have only one or two sets of wrinkles to overcome, such as on the forehead or around the eyes. This procedure would only take a few minutes. If you do more than one exercise, wait about one minute between each exercise.

We will work on seventeen buttons to eliminate wrinkles on the entire face. Let us start with the wrinkles on the forehead.

Forehead. Looking at Photo 64, press to relax buttons 1 and 3 for two minutes each, using fingers on both hands simultaneously. (Be sure to time this with your watch.) Then, with the light tapping of your fingertips, tonify point 3 for thirty seconds.

When I tell you to relax a button for so many minutes, remember always to use the ten-second press and the ten-second pause for the minutes indicated, unless otherwise directed.

Bridge of Nose. Wait one minute before treating the bridge of the nose between the eyes. Using the same method as you did on the forehead, press the fingers on buttons 2 and 6, hold for two or three minutes. Remember to pause for ten seconds and press for ten seconds. Tonify button 3 with light tapping of your fingertips for one minute.

Upper Eyelids. To help erase wrinkles of the upper eyelids and the eyebrow area, tonify buttons 3 and 4 for two and one-half minutes each. Remember, this involves light tapping only.

Outer Corners of Eyes. Relax buttons 5, 8, and 15 for about three minutes each, then tonify button 3 for sixty to ninety seconds.

Wrinkles beneath the Eyes. For wrinkles beneath the eyes, *tonify only* buttons 7 and 8 for one minute each.

Face Wrinkles. For wrinkles running from the outer corners of your eyes to your jaw, relax buttons 1 and 15 for three minutes and tonify buttons 14 and 17 for one minute each.

Wrinkles to Jaw. For wrinkles running from the bridge of your nose under your eyes and down to your jaw, relax button 15 for three minutes and tonify buttons 14 and 17 for one minute.

Wrinkles around Mouth. For wrinkles that run from your nostrils around your mouth, relax buttons 10 and 15 for three minutes and tonify buttons 14 and 17 for one minute.

Sides of Mouth Wrinkles. To vanish wrinkles around the sides of your mouth, relax buttons 14, 15, and 16 for two to three minutes each and tonify button 11 for one minute.

Upper Lip Wrinkles. To get rid of the wrinkles between your nose and upper lip, you will relax buttons 13 and 14 three minutes each and tonify buttons 11, 12, and 15 for about thirty seconds.

Lower Lip and Chin. To control the wrinkles between your lower lip and chin, relax buttons 16 and 17 for three minutes each and tonify button 14 for one minute.

Now, you have covered all of the face muscles to give you an easy and simple at-home face lift, and no one need be the wiser. It will take some of your time, but think how rewarding it will be when your friends start asking you what you have done to look so young! When you use my special exotic aloe vera moisturizing lotions along with the special face lift, you will have a million-dollar secret to keep you young-looking and beautiful the rest of your life.

Pulling Ears for Beauty

I have explained in the chapter on ears how beneficial it is to pull on the ears to help stimulate many organs and glands, especially those that influence the skin. See Photos 18, 19, and 20.

Reflexes to Hormone-Producing Glands

Place your thumbs just under both sides of the chin. See Photo 25. Here is where the energy bottles up and causes you to lose all ambition (and forms double chins). With your thumbs hooked under your chin, work on your lymph nodes to make this area soft and pliable. This will increase both energy and the flow of hormones. The skin will be able to breathe so you will have healthier skin with wrinkles gone and less need for cosmetics. Your skin will also be easier to shave. Press in with the thumbs, and milk these glands toward the chin. Do this one at a time about three times on each side.

The next method of reflex massage helps even quite elderly ladies and men remain wrinkle-free and beautiful. Place the thumb on one side of the esophagus (throat) and the fingers on the opposite side. See Photo 32. Starting under the chin, press and massage with a rolling motion all the way to the collarbone. Then change hands and do it with the opposite thumb and fingers. Do this three times with each hand. Now use the same procedure, only start at the collarbone and massage toward the chin three times with each hand. This also will stimulate the production of hormones, giving you a beautiful skin.

A TOUCH FOR BEAUTY

See the numbered reflex buttons on the face in Photo 65. With the ring finger, start on number 1 at the top of the forehead. With a gentle, rolling pressure, massage this reflex for the count of three, then repeat the procedure with numbers 2 and 3. For numbers 4, 5, and 6, use the fingers of both hands simultaneously. Continue with one finger on 7, 8, and 9. Do this twice a day when you are cleaning your face, and let it become a habit, to stimulate beauty and health-producing hormones throughout the body.

I have given you several ways to help regain a beautiful skin and to keep it healthy and beautiful the rest of your life by using the touch of your fingertips. Always remember your true beauty comes from within, no matter what methods you use to beautify your body on the outside. If your heart is filled with envy, hate, jealousy, and ugly, unhappy thoughts, it will discolor your aura for all to see.

What you thought yesterday, you will live today; what you think today, you will live tomorrow. If you want to live a life filled with health and beauty, joy and happiness, then think *only* of that which is beautiful! And you *will* be *beautiful*.

HELP FOR ACNE

The heartbreak of many a young developing boy and girl is acne, the problems of which sometimes, psychologically, last into their adult life. Acne is not cured from the outside alone. You must treat the cause, and diet is at the root of the cause. You need to eat lots of raw vegetables and fruits instead of starches and sugars. Take lots of vitamins A, C, and the B vitamins. Get lots of good hard exercise to get oxygen into the bloodstream.

The trampoline is especially good to get oxygen circulating through every cell in your body. The miniature trampoline called the rebounder is described in this book in the chapter on using reflex devices.

Use reflex massage on all the reflexes to the endocrine glands, to stimulate oil and hormones into the skin. See Diagram 5. Remember, a healthy body means a healthy skin and a beautiful complexion.

I am going to give you a sure-cure for acne, for getting at the cause on the inside. This is a recipe using brewer's yeast, which abounds in B vitamins. Start with a small amount and increase it up to the amount in the recipe.

Recipe: Take one to two tablespoons of brewer's yeast, which can be found at the health food store (not baker's yeast), one to two tablespoons lecithin or two lecithin capsules (I like to use the capsules), one tablespoon cold pressed oil, safflower oil preferred. Take with milk, nonfat dry milk, or apple juice. Do not use orange or grapefruit juice. If you wish a sweetener in this, do not use sugar but a substitute. I like to use blackstrap molasses, which not only sweetens but also is filled with minerals and is healthy for you. Take this every morning and add vitamins and calcium. If you stay with this recipe and don't neglect taking it every day, this will not only turn you into a human dynamo of energy and happiness, it will also reward you with a beautiful, clear complexion and glossy healthy hair. If you go on a trip, a long one or just overnight, take your brewer's yeast with you.

I would advise you to use only pure soaps. (I never use soap on my face.) You might want to use my special skin lotions which are developed from aloe vera and vitamin E to help develop and keep a silky smooth complexion the rest of your life.

25

How to Use Reflexology for Beautiful and Healthy Hair

The health of your hair reflects the health of your body. It is the frame for your face and influences the picture others see, be it beautiful or ordinary. When I used to paint, I would take the finished painting to a frame shop and fit the frame to the picture. It is amazing what a frame will do to bring out the beauty of a painting and how the wrong frame can completely ruin the beauty of the same painting. After you develop beautiful hair, be sure and have it styled to frame the special beauty of your face.

ENERGIZING HAIR ROOTS

The first thing to do to energize the hair roots is to grab handfuls of hair and pull. Ouch! See Photo 1. Do this over the whole head. As you pull and yank it gently, you will feel as if your head is coming alive. This feeling will last several minutes. Look at Diagrams 2, 3, and 4 to become aware of how many gland and organ reflexes are being stimulated as you do this exercise. This is also said to help a hangover, indigestion, and other complaints.

To further stimulate these reflexes in the head, lightly close your hands into loose fists. With a loose wrist action, lightly pound the whole head. See Photo 2. This will not only stimulate the hair but also the brain, bladder, liver, and many other organs in the body. Look at Photo 3 where a wire brush is being used to tap the reflexes in the head to add even greater electrical stimulation to the hair and many other parts of the body.

Now, we will turn to the miraculous method of buffing the nails. See Photo 16. Place the fingernails of one hand against the fingernails of the other hand and buff them together. Buff, faster and faster, until you are making them sing. After doing this a few moments, stop and hold the hands relaxed. Feel the buildup of electrical energy in the hands. When you relax, you feel this powerful force stimulating your whole body.

HOW TO MASSAGE REFLEXES TO THE HAIR

Mr. D. came to see me after using the nail buffing for a few weeks to regrow hair. Mr. D. told me that he had a very hard time getting up in the mornings. It seemed that his energy had all drained out during the night; he had been this way for many years. Since he was quite bald, he decided to try my suggested method of buffing his nails. He decided that the best time to do this was in the morning before he got out of bed. He would buff his nails for five minutes every morning and then hop out of bed full of pep and energy. One day, it dawned on him that buffing his nails was stimulating not only his hair but his whole body. He says that he has never again had trouble getting up and happily showed me a new growth of hair on his head. He was very proud. He told me about his mother-in-law who was quite elderly. She had very white hair and had tried the same treatment. He said that she had also regained a lot of her old energy but that her pretty white hair was all turning dark on the back of her head.

For beautiful hair, you must keep it clean by shampooing often. Aloe vera and jojobo are very good to help keep the hair beautiful and healthy. Vinegar is still a good rinse. Always wash your comb and brush when you wash your hair, and make sure you use a large comb with wide space between the teeth so that it will not stretch and break the hair. I also use a wire brush, which not only stimulates the hair but tends to go through the hair without disturbing the hairstyle.

STIMULATING HAIR FOLLICLES

Let us look a little further into stimulating the hair follicle. This is for those who have lost their hair and for those who find their hair thinning in certain spots.

Place your first two fingers in front of the upper half of the ears on the bony structure of the head. We know that the hair needs stimulation to be healthy, but mainly it needs blood. You are going to push the blood up into the roots of the hair with your fingertips. Press hard enough to feel the blood being forced up into the scalp. Do this several times, working toward the front and then toward the middle of the head and then clear around to the back. Start this slowly and not too hard at first or you might start a headache.

Now you know all there is to know about having a beautiful head of hair. With a diet rich in vitamins and minerals (especially zinc), and lots of vegetables and fruit, you can have the healthiest, most beautiful hair in town.

26

How to Take Care of and Develop Beautiful Breasts

The breasts are important to a woman's self-confidence. She has been conscious of her breasts from the time she was a child. The breasts represent her femininity, and she watches the development of these organs with pride just as a boy watches the development of his reproductive organs.

Not every woman ends up with the beautiful, full, rounded breasts that she would like to have. By using the magic massage of reflexology, you can have the lovely, full, rounded breasts of your youth.

MASSAGING THE BREASTS

Place both of your hands on the bare breasts, left hand on left breast, right hand on right breast. Using your hands as cups, fingers pointing toward the breastbone, thumbs pointing up with nipples protruding between the thumb and index fingers, gently massage with a rotary motion as you lift the breasts while sliding the fingers up toward the throat.

Start with the fingers far enough back so that you can feel the pull on the muscles under the arms. Use a forward lifting massage with each rotation. Do not do this very often, at first, or you will have some pretty sore breasts.

Dr. Popov taught us to use the above method of developing the breasts in his rejuvenation center, having us pour sea salts over the breasts as we massaged them.

One young woman there had had silicone injected into her breasts to make them larger, but she complained that they felt uncomfortable and bothered her a lot. Dr. Popov assured her she would not need the added silicone if she followed faithfully the reflex massage of the breasts as directed.

MASSAGING REFLEXES

When you are massaging reflexes in your neck for a beautiful skin, you are also stimulating hormones to help in the development of the breasts. See Photo 32.

Since the breasts are related to the sex glands, you will be stimulating the breasts even more as you massage the reflexes to the gonads and the endocrine glands as explained in other chapters. See also Diagrams 18A, C, and D.

Kneading and massaging the breasts with the fingers and palms will enlarge them and help them keep their shape.

REVERSING MASSAGE

Reverse the massage by placing the fingers of the left hand on the breastbone and sliding them under the right breast, working the fingers clear around the breast with an uplifting motion. See Photo 66. Do this several times, and use the same massage on the left breast. I learned this technique in the Philippines from a vein doctor: Place the fingers of the right hand on the breastbone between the breasts as before, but here, follow a vein *under* the breast, pressing on the solid bone. Work the fingers around the breast clear around the outer edge and on up into the fore part of the arm. The next time around, follow this procedure but massage on up toward the outer muscle of the arm. See Diagram 18A. At first, you may find some very tender spots as you do these breast massages. The doctor claims you are cleaning out old, stagnated blood, and it is true. Very soon you will not find any tender places in or around the breasts. If you should feel any unduly tender spots in the breasts that do not go away, be sure to check with a doctor.

Something to remember is that tests in a university study of forty-seven women revealed that 65 percent of the women were able to dissolve their benign breast lumps and avoid biopsy. All they did was alter their diet. According to Dr. John Minton, all that is necessary is to give up coffee, tea, chocolate, and cola, which contain stimulants

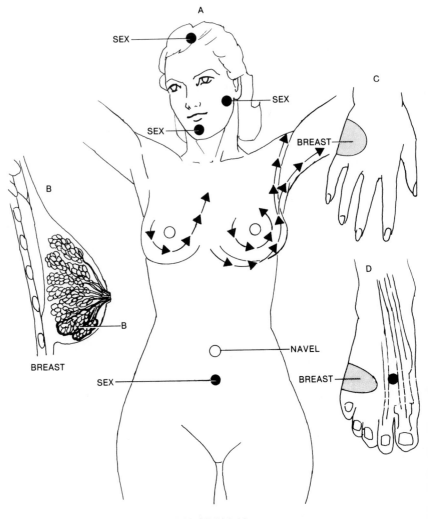

DIAGRAM 18

Notice in the diagram of the breast
how the lactiferous (milk-produc-
ing) glands and ducts flow toward
the nipple. B shows a cross-section
of gland and duct; C and D show
breast-stimulating reflex points.

known as methylxanthines. He says that these stimulants apparently provoke the growth of cystic lumps.

Now, one more breast massage: Place the fingers of the left hand on the nipple of the left breast and slowly massage toward the outer part of the body in a circle. Keep enlarging the circle until you are covering the entire breast. This may be done with the flat of the hand also. Do the other breast the same way.

Conclusion
Heal Thyself and Thy Neighbor

In this book, I have given you several natural methods of healing from the very simplest headache to the most serious of chronic degenerative diseases.

I have not written this book for you to read and cast aside. I want you to put it to daily use for yourself, your loved ones, and your neighbors.

I have devoted my life to research so that I might be able to bring every man, woman, child, and even animal a natural, simple, harmless way to live a life free from pain and illness, safe and free! I want you to understand and learn to use God's most precious gift, *reflexology*, nature's way to perfect health.

It would be impossible for me to reveal in one book all of the miraculous methods of natural healing that I have discovered in my many years of research throughout the world.

I can truthfully say that in all of my traveling and research, here and abroad, I have never found any method of healing that can compare with the simple dynamic healing power of reflexology.

Although I have given you a few other methods of natural healing to use along with reflexology, I want you to know that reflexology is the primary key to natural healing of every illness and freedom from pain when used as directed.

Although this book deals mostly with physical and material aspects of gaining health and freedom from pain, keep in mind that the real purpose of attaining a healthy, long life is to recognize the higher divine purpose for which we were born. Perfect health would be wasted unless the healthy body is used as a temple for our spirit to develop in. Our life on this planet is a schooling period to enable us to improve and perfect our human and divine characteristics.

Through the directions given in this book and my previous books on foot and hand reflexology, you may use this dynamic power of natural healing for yourself and for those who are crying out in anguished suffering and despair—by the simple method of pressing certain electrical reflex buttons located throughout the body. Although different bodies require different medication and vitamins, *reflexology works the same for all bodies.*

I have given you the key to the source and the power to heal. Open the door, step in, and heal thy neighbor and thyself.

Index